New Clinical Concepts in Marital Therapy

CLINICAL INSIGHTS

New Clinical Concepts in Marital Therapy

Edited by
OLIVER J. W. BJORKSTEN, M.D.

Associate Professor of Psychiatry and Behavioral Sciences,
Medical University of South Carolina, Charleston

AMERICAN PSYCHIATRIC PRESS, INC.
Washington, D.C.

© 1985 American Psychiatric Association

Manufactured in the U.S.A.

The paper used in this publication meets the minimum requirements of American National Standard for Information Sciences—Permanence of Paper for Printed Library Materials, ANSI Z39.48-1984. ∞™

Library of Congress Cataloging in Publication Data

Main entry under title:

New clinical concepts in marital therapy.

    (Clinical insights)
    Includes bibliographies.
      1. Married people—Mental health—Addresses, essays, lectures.
2. Marital status—Psychological aspects—Addresses, essays, lectures.
3. Marriage—United States—Addresses, essays, lectures.   4. Marital psychotherapy—Addresses, essays, lectures.
I. Bjorksten, Oliver J. W., 1942–   .   II. Series. [DNLM: 1. Marital Therapy. WM 55 N532]
RC488.5.N496   1985   616.89′156   85-11201
ISBN 0-88048-074-2 (pbk.)

Contents

Introduction vii
Oliver J. W. Bjorksten, M.D.

**1 Sociodemographic Aspects
of Contemporary
American Marriage** 1
Thomas J. Stewart, Ph.D.
Oliver J. W. Bjorksten, M.D.
Ira D. Glick, M.D.

**2 Marital Status and
Psychiatric Morbidity** 57
R. Taylor Segraves, M.D., Ph.D.

3 Marital Status and Health 81
Oliver J. W. Bjorksten, M.D.
Thomas J. Stewart, Ph.D.

4 Second Marriages 111
Clifford J. Sager, M.D.

**5 An Integrative Approach
to Couples Therapy** 151
Derek C. Polonsky, M.D.
Carol C. Nadelson, M.D.

Contributors

OLIVER J. W. BJORKSTEN, M.D.
Associate Professor of Psychiatry and Behavioral Sciences,
Medical University of South Carolina, Charleston

IRA D. GLICK, M.D.
Professor of Psychiatry, Department of Psychiatry; and
Associate Medical Director, Payne Whitney Psychiatric Clinic,
The New York Hospital–Cornell Medical Center, New York

CAROL C. NADELSON, M.D.
President, American Psychiatric Association; Professor and Vice-Chairman,
and Director of Training and Education,
Tufts–New England Medical Center, Boston

DEREK C. POLONSKY, M.D.
Assistant Clinical Professor of Psychiatry,
Tufts–New England Medical Center, Boston

CLIFFORD J. SAGER, M.D.
Clinical Professor of Psychiatry, The New York Hospital–Cornell Medical
Center; Director of Family Psychiatry, Jewish Board of Family and Children's
Services, New York

R. TAYLOR SEGRAVES, M.D., PH.D.
Professor of Psychiatry, Tulane University, New Orleans

THOMAS J. STEWART, PH.D.
Chairman, Department of Health Services Administration,
Medical University of South Carolina, Charleston

Introduction

In 1785, the *New York Daily Advertiser* published a survey of 868,742 couples and reported that 1,102 were "reputedly happy in the esteem of the world," 135 were "comparatively happy," and only nine were "absolutely and entirely happy" (1). Regardless of its scientific validity, this report indicates that American readers at that time were interested in marriage. This fascination has continued to the present.

Early in our history, immigrants seeking escape from religious and social restrictions brought European marital customs to this country, customs that have gradually evolved into our own unique forms of marriage. The goals of "life, liberty, and the pursuit of happiness" were even incorporated into the Declaration of Independence. It should not be surprising that marriage in America has evolved in accordance with these principles, to become a unique institution in the world because it is based primarily on love and, in comparison with other countries, freedom, especially the freedom to leave the marital relationship. Marriage continues to evolve, and currently our ideal companionate form of marriage is largely due to the continuing increase in women's status.

Today, we acknowledge and accept people's right to adjust their marriages to suit their changing needs. Associated with this attitude, whether cause or effect, are high levels of marital activity—that is, marriage, divorce, and remarriage—which has resulted in fundamental changes in the nature of marriage itself. We view marriage as *less permanent* than before, as an institution designed to be *fulfilling*, and one in which *each person has reciprocal* rights and obligations. The form of marriage has changed, since today there are large numbers of reconstituted families due to remarriage.

Marriage is, and always has been, a pervasive institution in this country; the vast majority of Americans will marry at some time in their lives. If divorce occurs, the majority will remarry. Thus, it is vital for psychiatrists to understand the social context of marriage, since it represents such an important aspect of our patients' lives. Marriage can either be protective, in the sense that it reduces stress and illness, or it can be stressful, either by conflict within it or by its disruption.

The purpose of this monograph is to review a few selected aspects of marriage that are of current relevance to the psychiatrist. Much of this material was presented at a symposium held at the Annual Meeting of the American Psychiatric Association in May 1984.

Chapter 1, by Drs. Stewart, Bjorksten, and Glick, reviews current trends in marriage from a statistical point of view. Marital statistics are frequently bandied about, especially in the lay press, in order to demonstrate whatever point of view the author wishes to promulgate. Our review of marital statistics indicates that marital phenomena are quite complex and frequently interrelated. It is necessary to take both a historical perspective in order to understand how various aspects of marriage have evolved over time, and an interactive perspective in order to see the interrelationships of marital trends. For example, examination of divorce rates alone might lead one to the erroneous conclusion that there is a greater degree of marital disruption today than in the past, and that therefore people are more disillusioned by the institution of marriage itself. Careful examination of trends in marital disruption and remarriage refutes both of these ideas.

Marital disruption does have psychiatric and physical consequences that will be reviewed in Chapters 2 and 3. Dr. Segraves reviews the literature relating marital status to psychiatric morbidity in Chapter 2. This is particularly pertinent for psychiatrists, since Dr. Segraves clearly demonstrates that there is an overrepresentation of divorced persons in both psychiatric inpatient and outpatient facilities. Whether this is a cause or an effect of their change in marital status is an interesting question, one which he addresses here. In Chapter 3, Drs. Bjorksten and Stewart examine the relationship of morbidity and mortality to marital disruption and propose a number of mechanisms to account for these associations.

The enormously high remarriage rate today has led to a vast increase in the reconstituted family, which represents a complex and little-studied psychiatric phenomenon. This new family environment suggests new developmental forces on children as well as essentially new kinds of marital dynamics and pathology. This area is reviewed by Dr. Sager in Chapter 4, where the clinical implications are elaborated.

In recent years, the treatment of marital problems has received greater attention by psychiatrists, and proponents of various forms of psychotherapy have begun to apply their own theoretical concepts to this form of treatment. These initiatives have been occurring inconspicuously, since they represent some departures from standard practice. Recently, it has become apparent that practitioners are integrating various treatment approaches in their work with couples. This integration has important implications with respect not only to marital but also to individual psychotherapy. Drs. Polanski and Nadelson review some of these integrative concepts with respect to marital therapy in Chapter 5.

This monograph is not a textbook of marital therapy, but rather is an attempt to inform the reader about some currently important areas in American marriage. For a fuller treatment of each of these areas and of therapeutic concepts in marital therapy, the reader is referred to primary sources.

Oliver J. W. Bjorksten, M.D.

Reference

1. Murstein BI: Love, Sex and Marriage Through the Ages. New York, Springer Publishing Co., 1974

1

Sociodemographic Aspects of Contemporary American Marriage

Thomas J. Stewart, Ph.D.
Oliver J. W. Bjorksten, M.D.
Ira D. Glick, M.D.

1

Sociodemographic Aspects of Contemporary American Marriage

Patients' cultural and familial environment is a critical component in the clinical appraisal of psychiatric disability. Traditionally, "work and love" were key concepts in the psychoanalytic evaluation of mental health, and they continue to be an important standard of success in personal adjustment. However, the appraisal of love, often in terms of marital relationships, must be taken in social and cultural context. It is vital for psychiatrists to have a basic understanding of current and evolving norms, patterns, and trends in American marriage to aid in the assessment of their patients. This chapter will offer an overview and synthesis of contemporary American marital trends in a historical context as well as a discussion of their clinical implications.

In the past, marital status was usually viewed as binary; that is, one was either married or not, and the state of marriage, once assumed, was felt to be essentially permanent. Today it appears that marital status has assumed a cyclical pattern, with frequent shifts in marital status from marriage to divorce and finally to remarriage. This marital pool activity makes the understanding of marital phenomena complex, since it is impossible to obtain an accurate picture from individual statistics, such as the divorce rate, alone. In this review we will attempt to integrate statistics in both a historical and a functional fashion.

We use the term marriage in its broadest and most generic sense. Murstein (1) defines marriage as "a socially legitimate sexual union, begun with a public announcement and undertaken with some idea of permanence; it is undertaken with a more or less explicit contract which spells out rights and obligations between spouses and between spouses and future children." We agree with this definition, although it does not include such categories of individuals as those who are living together or, in many cases, reconstituted families. Divorce is defined as a legal and behavioral dissolution of marriage, and remarriage is defined as the marriage of individuals who have been previously married.

HISTORICAL TRENDS

Contemporary observers from both the political right and the left refer to the happy, extended, multigenerational family of bygone times as the ideal to which we should aspire, and they lament the current "dismal" state of family life as though we have somehow fallen from grace. While some attribute this fall to moral decay, others blame governmental intrusion into private and family matters. All agree, however, that things were seemingly better in the past and that family life today is deteriorating. Frequently, the increasing divorce rate is taken as a single measure of this family disintegration and is interpreted as a sign that marriage is no longer important to Americans. Television versions of family life facilitate this mythic image by portraying families in the past as long-lived, multigenerational, geographically stable, and healthy. Men and women are shown as being family oriented, while the current view is that women, in particular, are less interested in becoming married and much less interested in bearing children.

A historical review of marital data reveals that the above assumptions are largely inaccurate. One of the most striking findings of such a review is that a number of marital patterns that were common in the past continue to be prevalent today. The nuclear family, including two generations, continues to be the basic family unit in European and American societies as it has been over the last several centuries. Laslett (2), Shorter (3), and

Demos (4) have demonstrated this constancy in western Europe and the United States. In the past, very few American families (about 7 percent to 8 percent) had more than three generations living in the same household, and this percentage has remained constant (4). Thus, the multigenerational extended family represented only an ideal which in fact occurred in only a small minority of our population. Factors such as the migration to frontier lands, high mortality, and varying economic conditions have all adversely affected the availability and stability of multigenerational families. Indeed, the substantial number of three- and

Table 1. Percentages Ever-Married and Childless, and Mean Number of Children per Mother, Women Born 1846–1940, by Birth Cohort

Year of Birth of Women	Census Year	Age at Survey	Total No. of Women	Percent Ever-Married	Percent Childless among Ever-married	Average No. of Children per Woman with Children
	Data Source					
1846–1855	1910	55–64	2,385	92.7	8.2	5.71
1856–1865	1910	45–54	3,868	91.3	9.2	5.33
1866–1975	1910	35–44	5,500	88.4	11.1	4.55
	1940	65–74	3,173	90.4	13.2	4.35
1876–1885	1940	55–64	5,122	91.0	15.2	4.02
1866–1890	1940	50–54	3,469	91.3	15.2	3.75
1891–1895	1940	45–49	3,987	91.4	15.4	3.62
1896–1900	1940	40–44	4,271	90.2	16.2	3.30
	1950	50–54	4,077	92.3	18.6	3.32
1901–1905	1950	45–49	4,480	92.0	20.4	3.13
1906–1910	1950	40–44	5,083	91.8	20.0	2.96
	1960	50–54	4,927	92.4	20.6	2.97
1911–1915	1960	45–49	5,560	93.5	18.2	2.94
1916–1920	1960	40–44	5,898	93.9	14.1	2.99
	1970	50–54	5,735	94.3	13.8	3.02
1921–1925	1970	45–49	6,250	94.7	10.6	3.20
1926–1930	1970	40–44	6,154	94.0	8.6	3.39
1931–1935	1970	35–39	5,711	94.1	7.3	3.42
1936–1940	1970	30–34	5,852	92.6	8.3	3.06

Calculated from U.S. Census, 1940: Differential fertility 1940 and 1910, Tables 1–6; U.S. Census, 1950: Fertility, Tables 1, 2, and 16; U.S. Census, 1960: Women by number of children ever born, Tables 1, 2, 3, 16, and 17; and U.S. Census, 1970: Women by number of children ever born, Table 8 (5).

four-generation families is a phenomenon primarily of the 20th century that is due to recent increases in longevity. Historical information about aging and mortality will be discussed below.

One of the most significant marital constants is the percentage of women who choose to marry and the percentage who become mothers. Table 1 reflects data collected on cohorts of women over roughly a 100-year period in American history and demonstrates that, although there are some minor fluctuations, women born in the period of 1936–1940 married and had children with approximately the same frequency as women did 100 years earlier. This constancy is remarkable, since during the last century there have been enormous cultural changes, wars, political and economic fluctuations, and alterations in health status. Regardless of these cultural shifts, the vast majority of women continue to enter marriage and bear children, thus demonstrating the viability of marriage as an institution.

The use of divorce data alone to indict marriage and to explain its dissolution is fraught with error. Marital dissolution can occur by three methods: divorce, desertion, and death. Table 2 indicates that during the past century the overall marital dissolution rate has remained remarkably constant. While the divorce rate has substantially increased, this trend has been offset by the dramatically falling death rate, leading to an overall marital dissolution rate of approximately 34 per 1,000 existing marriages. It is noteworthy that even with the increasing divorce rate, the majority of marriages today continue to end by the death of a spouse. Only 44 percent of all marriages in 1970 ended by divorce.

A key concept in the myth of the golden era of family life is that of geographic stability. We developed the image of a three-generation family living in a little house with a white picket fence. Although this concept may have a degree of validity for some European populations, it is dubious in the United States. Over the last 200 years the population of the United States has migrated westward to fill the entire continent. Geographic mobility has been and continues to be a way of life with Americans. The movement from rural to urban areas has been an important migration of this century, and migration continues today, primarily to the west and south (7). One of the standard American solutions to personal economic difficulties is to seek the pot of gold

Table 2. Annual Marital Dissolutions by Death and Legal Divorce, and Rates per 1,000 Existing Marriages, 1863–1970

Year	Dissolutions per year		Rates per 1,000 existing marriages			Divorces percent of total dissolution
	Deaths	Divorces	Deaths	Divorces	Combined	
1863–64	197,200	7,170	32.1	1.2	33.3	3.5
1865–69	207,000	10,529	31.1	1.6	32.7	4.8
1870–74	226,400	12,417	30.3	1.7	32.0	5.2
1875–79	238,600	15,574	28.7	1.9	30.6	6.1
1880–84	285,400	21,747	30.6	2.3	33.0	7.1
1885–89	290,400	27,466	27.6	2.6	30.2	8.6
1890–94	334,800	36,123	28.3	3.1	31.3	9.7
1895–99	328,800	45,462	24.9	3.4	28.4	12.1
1900–04	390,800	61,868	26.5	4.2	30.6	13.7
1905–09	427,400	74,626	25.4	4.4	29.8	14.9
1910–14	453,600	91,695	23.7	4.8	28.5	16.8
1915–19	551,000	119,529	26.0	5.6	31.6	17.8
1920–24	504,200	164,917	21.9	7.2	29.0	24.6
1925–29	573,200	193,218	22.6	7.6	30.3	25.2
1930–34	590,800	183,441	21.9	6.8	28.7	23.7
1935–39	634,600	239,600	21.9	8.3	30.2	27.4
1940–44	656,400	330,557	20.4	10.3	30.7	33.5
1945–49	681,200	485,641	19.2	13.7	32.8	41.6
1950–54	692,400	385,429	18.2	10.0	28.3	35.9
1955–59	733,600	385,385	18.3	9.2	27.8	34.2
1960–64	n.a.	419,600	n.a.	9.6	n.a.	n.a.
1965–69	n.a.	544,800	n.a.	11.7	n.a.	n.a.
1960	790,400	393,000	18.9	9.4	28.3	33.2
1961	789,200	414,000	18.7	9.8	28.6	34.4
1965	820,800	479,000	18.5	10.8	29.4	36.9
1970	908,200	715,000	19.3	15.2	34.5	44.0

Reprinted from Davis K: The American family in relation to demographic change, in Demographic and Social Aspects of Population Growth, Vol. 1. Edited by Westoff CF, Parke R. Washington, D.C., U.S. Government Printing Office, 1972 (6).

at the other end of the rainbow, which usually requires a geographic relocation. In our view, the goals of gold rush prospectors of the last century did not differ substantially from those of people who migrated out of the dust bowl during the depression or from those of people who sought economic opportunities in the oil-based communities of the southwest.

In summary, some facets of American marriage are strikingly consistent, including the percentage of women who marry and who have children, the rate of marital disruption, and the patterns of geographic mobility. On the other hand, there are important and striking changes in various aspects of marriage.

CURRENT MARITAL TRENDS

The most important single change in American society is the aging of the population. This aging can be viewed from two perspectives: life expectancy and trends in age distribution of the population. Life expectancy in the United States has increased substantially: In 1900 the average life expectancy was 49.2 years, but by 1983 it had climbed to 74.6 years (8). Figure 1 depicts the linear increase in life expectancy for both men and women, starting in 1950 and continuing, by projection, to the year 2000. As is well known, this increase in life expectancy is due to many factors, including improved nutrition, public health measures, and to a lesser extent, availability of and improvements in medical technology. As death rates fall, there is usually a secondary decline in birth rates due to changes in the perceived value of having many children and the wish to maintain the high quality of life that is often threatened by large families. The paired phenomena of dropping death rates followed by dropping birth rates is known as the *demographic transition*. The demographic transition in America started in the earlier part of the century and is continuing today.

As life expectancy improves, it is followed by increases in survivability, which means that larger cohorts of individuals remain alive into their later years. As a consequence of the demographic transition, in which larger numbers of people survive and

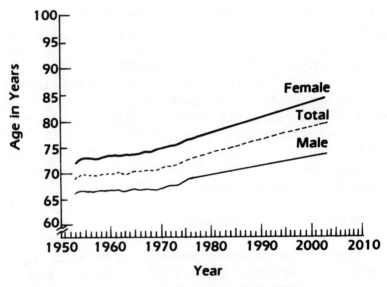

Figure 1. Life expectancy in the United States, 1950–2003.

From Rice DP: Projection and analysis of health status trends. Paper presented at the 106th Annual Meeting of the American Public Health Association, Los Angeles, October 1978 (9). Published by permission.

fewer are born, there is a massive redistribution of the age structure of the American population. This is portrayed in Figure 2 in which it will be observed that by the year 2050 more than 20 percent of the population will be over the age of 65, and approximately 30 percent of the population will be under the age of 25. This redistribution will have an enormous impact on economics, politics, health care, and marriage. Psychiatrists in the future can expect to see many older patients and will be faced with the clinical management of more age-related diseases such as dementia.

A variation on the theme of declining mortality in this century is the sex differential in mortality, that is, the difference between male and female life expectancy. It is interesting that the survivability of women has improved more than that of men since 1900. In that year, the differential favoring women was 2.9 years, whereas in 1983 women lived 7.4 years longer than men did (8).

The impact of changes in life expectancy and of the sex differential in mortality can be seen in terms of changing patterns in widowhood and the frequency of multigenerational families. Figure 3 demonstrates that after the middle years of life the sex differential in mortality leads to vastly greater numbers of widows than of widowers. Figure 4 shows that correspondingly fewer women than men are married after the age of 44 (because of the deaths of their husbands). The family circumstances of men and women are poignantly illustrated in Table 3, which shows that as of 1982, 80 percent of men over the age of 65 were married, while only 40 percent of women were. Of greater significance is that while 83.7 percent of these older men were living in families, only 56.8 percent of the women were.

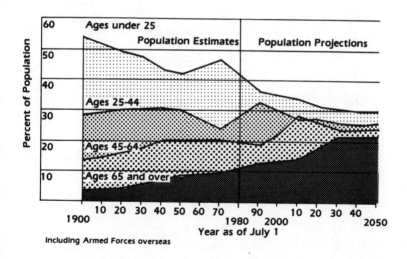

Figure 2. Trend in age distribution of United States population, 1900–2050.

From various reports (10) and unpublished data of the Bureau of the Census. Washington, D.C., U.S. Dept. of Health and Human Services, Series 21, No. 25, p. 7, December 1973.

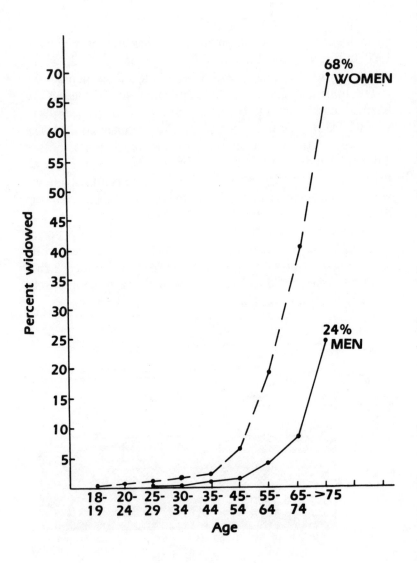

Figure 3. Percentage of widowed men and women by age groups.

Reprinted from U.S. Statistical Report, Table 49, p. 38. Washington, D.C., U.S. Government Printing Office, 1980 (11).

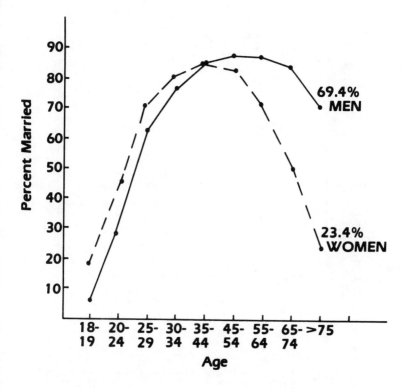

Figure 4. Percentage of married men and women by age groups.

Reprinted from U.S. Statistical Report, Table 49, p. 38. Washington, D.C., U.S. Government Printing Office, 1980 (11).

Thus, today it is clear that women are the survivors of marriage and that as they grow older they do not live in a family or marital situation with nearly the same frequency as men do. One of the reasons for this is that widowers tend to remarry more often than widows, as can be seen from Table 4. However, there have been some indications that older women are experimenting with alternative living arrangements (14). Of the 12,500,000 currently widowed individuals in the United States, approximately 2,000,000

Table 3. Characteristics of Population Aged 65 and Over in the United States, March 1982

Characteristics	Men			Women		
	Ages 65 and over	Ages 65–74	Ages 75 and over	Ages 65 and over	Ages 65–74	Ages 75 and over
Population (no. in thousands)	10,310	6,770	3,540	14,920	8,927	5,993
Race (%)						
White	90.0	89.7	90.6	90.5	90.1	91.2
All other	10.0	10.3	9.4	9.5	9.9	8.8
Marital status (%)						
Single	4.4	4.9	3.3	5.6	5.3	6.1
Married	80.0	84.0	72.5	40.2	51.3	23.6
Widowed	12.4	7.5	21.8	50.4	38.3	68.5
Divorced	3.2	3.6	2.4	3.8	5.1	1.8
Family status (%)						
In families	83.7	86.6	78.0	56.8	63.0	47.5
Householder	76.8	80.3	70.1	10.0	10.0	10.0
Married spouse present	73.9	78.0	66.1	1.7	2.3	.9
Spouse of householder	3.1	3.0	3.2	36.4	46.7	21.2
Other	3.8	3.3	4.9	10.4	6.3	16.3
Not in families	16.3	13.4	22.0	43.2	37.0	52.5
Householder	15.3	12.4	21.1	42.4	36.1	51.8
Other	1.0	1.0	.9	.8	.9	.7

Reprinted from U.S. Bureau of the Census, Statistical Bulletin 65-10, 1984 (12).

Table 4. Probability That a New Widow or Widower Will Remarry
(by Sex, Race, and Age)

	Widows		Widowers	
Age	White	Black	White	Black
20–24	.88	.51	.98	.84
25–34	.86	.25	.88	.70
35–44	.41	.23	.88	.43
45–54	.26	.07	.59	.25
55–64	.05	.06	.48	.21
65–74	.004	. . . [a]	.24	.10
75 +	. . . [a]	. . . [a]	.06	. . . [a]

[a] Probability is essentially zero.
Reprinted from Cleveland WP, Gianturco DT: Remarriage probability after widowhood: a retrospective method. Journal of Gerontology 31:99, 1976 (13).

are male and 10,500,000 are female (15). One of the health implications of these statistics, which will be more fully elaborated in another chapter, is that this transition of marital status greatly increases the risk of morbidity and death.

The other major impact of increases in life expectancy is on the composition of families, so that today we expect more multigenerational ones than existed in the past. As Brody (16) has observed, "it appears that the 'empty nest' period between the ages of 50 and 60 will, in the future, be filled by grandparents and that families will be occupied with caretaking of their elderly parents and grandparents." Clearly, this will affect family dynamics. From a child's developmental perspective, family life in which grandparents and great-grandparents fully participate may be considerably different from what it would be if they were not even present.

As greater numbers of people live to age 85 and beyond, their care becomes a major issue for their progeny. Not only is their day-to-day sustenance a family matter but so are their health care needs. Figures 5 and 6 demonstrate that older people use health care facilities much more than do younger ones. Coupled with this increased health care utilization is a diminished ability for the elderly to pay for it themselves due to the decrease in income after retirement. Health care costs per person are generally greater for the elderly because of the multiplicity and chronicity of their health problems.

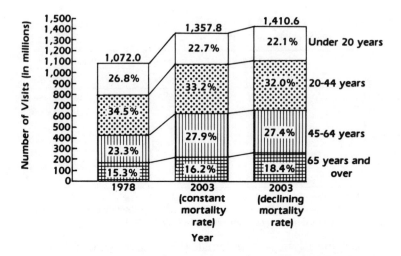

Figure 5. Projected number of physician visits and percentage distributions by age, in 1978 and 2003, in the United States (physician visits to hospital inpatients are not included).

From Rice DP: Projection and analysis of health status trends. Paper presented at the 106th Annual Meeting of the American Public Health Association, Los Angeles, October 1978 (9). Published by permission.

Although the majority of elderly people live with their families or by themselves, approximately 5 percent of them will be admitted to nursing homes and extended-care facilities. This change in living circumstances has a number of important implications. Helsing et al. (17) have demonstrated a substantial increase in mortality among elderly individuals who are institutionalized. Also, the decision to institutionalize the elderly can generate considerable guilt in their families. This decision usually symbolizes the family's acknowledgment of the elderly person's physical or mental deterioration, or both. Many families feel disloyal and fear that institutionalization of their parents and grandparents may be seen as trying to get rid of them. Our society does not seem to have

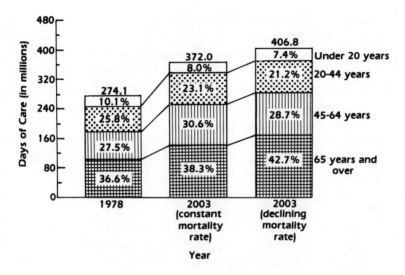

Figure 6. Projected days of care in nonfederal short-stay hospitals, and percentage distributions, by age, in 1978 and 2003, in the United States.

From Rice DP: Projection and analysis of health status trends. Paper presented at the 106th Annual Meeting of the American Public Health Association, Los Angeles, October 1978 (9). Published by permission.

a good mechanism that permits this ultimate and voluntary separation. Finally, greater survivability implies that more people than previously are experiencing family role reversal, that is, the son is becoming the father to the man. Childhood dependency will give way not only to adult autonomy and independence but to a caretaking role for the elderly as well. Although we have focused on the burdens of this role reversal, there may be some advantages too. Currently, the elderly often experience themselves as disenfranchised by our society. Their increased need for support may, in some ways, bring them closer and involve them more fully with mainstream American society. One may even argue that because of their increasing numbers they may come to enjoy much greater representation and influence upon our society.

Increased Status of Women

One of the most significant historical trends in marriage has been the gradual increase in the status of women. The nadir of women's status was probably in the year 585 when the council of Macon debated whether or not women had souls (1). Fortunately, the council concluded that women did, but by a plurality of only one vote! While progress in general has been slow, it is clear that from the time of the French Revolution onward, women's status has improved significantly. This trend is manifested in terms of at least two clearly measurable phenomena: employment and education.

Table 5 indicates that from 1890 to 1970 women increasingly participated in the labor force. Of particular interest is the proportion of single versus married women who work, and it can be seen that at the end of the last century and early in this one, most employed women were single. In general, a single woman would get a job only to quit upon marriage, and she usually would not reenter the labor force. By the end of World War II a reversal had taken place so that the majority of working women were married.

Table 5. Participation of Women in the Labor Force by Marital Status for the Years 1890–1970

Year	Percentage of total work force	Single	Married	Widowed or divorced
1890	18.2	68.2	13.9	17.9
1900	20.1	66.2	15.4	18.4
1910	n.a.	60.2	24.7	15.0
1920	22.7	77.0	23.0	n.a.
1930	23.6	53.9	28.9	17.2
1940	25.8	49.0	35.9	15.0
1950	29.9	31.9	52.2	16.0
1960	35.7	23.6	60.7	15.7
1970	41.4	22.5	62.3	15.0
1980	42.6	24.8	59.9	15.3

Adapted from U.S. Bureau of the Census: Historical Statistics of the United States. Washington, D.C., U.S. Government Printing Office, 1975 (18).

This suggests that although single women continue to work, their married compatriots rejoin the labor force later on. Today, women work prior to and often during the early years of marriage, leave the labor force temporarily during the childbearing and childrearing years, and then rejoin it.

Of interest is the constant proportion of widowed and divorced women in the labor force. It is to be recalled that there have been dramatic increases in the number of divorced individuals over the last hundred years as well as a dramatic increase in the number of women who are working. Thus, in 1890, 17.9 percent of the female work force was divorced, but that work force constituted only 18.2 percent of the total work force. In 1970, 15 percent of the female work force was divorced or widowed, but it represented 41.4 percent of the total work force, thus indicating huge increases in the actual number of divorced and widowed women who are employed. Whereas in 1980 women constituted approximately 40 percent of the total civilian labor force, the proportion of marriages in which both partners were employed doubled between 1960 and 1980 (15).

The educational status of women has been improving dramatically. In 1980, female students accounted for 50.6 percent of all college enrollments, an increase from the 34.5 percent reported in 1960 (15). The proportion of college or advanced degrees earned by women was 47.5 percent in 1980, up from 24.4 percent in 1950 (15). These figures dramatically underscore the increase in the education of women and strongly suggest that these highly educated women will be occupying top employment positions in the future. Figure 7 shows the dramatic increase in the proportion of women earning professional degrees. The major implication of the increased educational and employment status of women is that they are able to support themselves and thus are increasingly independent. This strongly suggests that women will feel less constrained by unwanted marital relationships and will be more capable of altering them. Murstein (1) has made the point that the increasing status of women not only leads to the possibility of love marriages but suggests higher divorce rates as well.

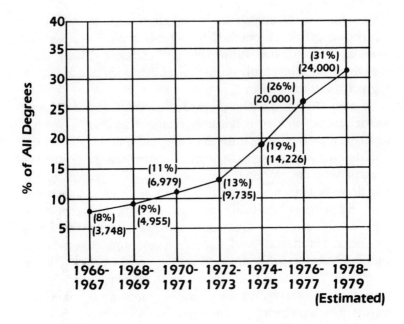

Figure 7. Percentage of Professional Degrees Awarded to Women, 1967–1979.

Women and Children

The vast majority of women continue to become mothers, although it appears that more women delay childbearing and prefer to have fewer children. In 1900, the average woman bore approximately six children, but today she usually has one or two. The number of children that a woman bears is affected by various factors including race, age, education, and presence in the labor force. Table 6 demonstrates that family size is related to race (white families are smaller), education (increase in number of

Table 6. Lifetime Births Expected by Wives, 18–34 Years Old, (Percentage Distribution), June 1979

Number of Births	Race			Age			Education			Labor Force Status	
	White	Black	Spanish origin[1]	18–24	25–29	30–34	Not high school graduate	High school graduate	College 1 year or more	In labor force	Not in labor force
None	5.8	4.2	3.5	5.2	5.3	6.4	3.6	5.2	7.3	8.2	2.5
One	12.3	14.0	8.5	11.8	12.9	12.6	11.3	12.3	13.3	15.3	8.9
Two	51.5	40.7	40.5	54.9	51.9	46.2	40.0	51.3	54.9	52.2	48.9
Three	21.4	23.3	28.1	20.9	21.3	22.4	26.1	22.8	17.8	17.7	26.5
Four or more	8.9	17.9	19.5	7.1	8.6	12.4	19.1	8.5	6.7	6.7	13.3

[1] Persons of Spanish origins may be of any race.
From U.S. Bureau of the Census, Current Population Reports, series P-20, No. 358, 1980, and earlier issues (20).

Table 7.   Conceptual Life Cycles (Mean Ages at Major Events) of Women in
Mid-19th and Mid-20th Centuries

	Year of Birth	
Event	1849–1855[a]	1946–1955[b]
First marriage	22.0	20.8
Birth of first child	23.5	22.3
Birth of last child	36.0	24.8
First marriage of last child	58.9	47.7
Death of spouse	56.4	67.7
Own death	60.7	77.1

[a] Mean number of children, six.
[b] Mean number of children, two.
Adapted from Bane MJ: Here to Stay. New York, Basic Books, 1978 (21).

years in school is related to smaller family size) and labor force
status (employed women have smaller families).

One of the most profound changes in the evolution of marriage
in the United States is the substantial modification of the life cycle
of women. The hypothetical life cycle is a conceptual construct
based upon the ages at which signal events in the family lives of
women occur. These ages are based upon mean years of age at
which these events occur for cohorts of women. The data can be
developed for historical cohorts and projected for contemporary
and future cohorts. Table 7 is a depiction of the life cycle events of
women who were born at the midpoints of the 19th and 20th
centuries. In a sense this table summarizes a number of the points
that have already been made regarding changes in women's aging
and status. Interestingly, the first marriage of women in these two
cohorts occurs at roughly the same time, with modern women
marrying at a slightly younger age. Roughly the same amount of
time passes until the birth of the first child. However, the first
major change is the amount of time spent in childbearing years.
Women born in the mid-19th century spent 12.5 years from the
birth of the first to last child. Modern women, on the other hand,
experience a corresponding period of only 2.5 years, with the
consequence that they end their childbearing responsibilities at a
much earlier age than women used to. This, coupled with their
greater longevity, defines a rather extensive period in which they

Table 8. Duration (in Years) of Women's Life Stages, 19th and 20th Centuries

Stage	Women born	
	1849–1855	1946–1955
1: First marriage to birth of first child	1.5	1.5
2: Birth of first child to birth of last child	12.5	2.5
3: Birth of last child to first marriage of last child	22.9	22.9
4: First marriage of last child to death of spouse	−2.9	20.0
5: Death of spouse to own death	4.3	9.4

Adapted from Bane MJ: Here to Stay. New York, Basic Books, 1978 (21).

will have no childrearing responsibilities and will therefore have an opportunity to spend more time with their spouse, that is, a postchildrearing marriage. These relationships can be seen in Table 8, which shows that postchildrearing marriage is a new phenomenon that lasts for an average of 20 years. In summary, the comparison of women from these two periods indicates that there has been a substantial truncation of childbearing years and a pronounced increase in postchildrearing years.

Today it seems reasonable, on the basis of this conceptual life cycle for men and women, to speak of essentially two marriages. The first might be referred to as a family-oriented marriage in which children are present, and the second as a postchildrearing marriage after the children have left home. It can be anticipated that women will spend at least 20 years in this postchildrearing marriage; the period will probably be shorter for men because of their earlier demise. Nevertheless, it will last long enough to represent a significant period of time and will give greater importance to the midlife transition. The adaptations and skills necessary for a successful family-oriented marriage cannot be assumed to apply necessarily in the postchildrearing one with its greater intimacy and couple orientation. The focus and function of the marriage shifts from one external, that is, children, to the relationship itself. The demand on the couple is to have fun and be happy, a task they may not be accustomed to or particularly adept at. The focus of counseling efforts with these couples is usually less on problem solving and more on the development of pleasurable activities and a more rewarding intimate relationship.

Patterns of Sexual Behavior

The sexual revolution in America, which began around 1960 and continues into the present, hardly warrants explanation. Many of the seemingly radical attitudes and behaviors of the 1960s have gradually come to be incorporated into everyday life in the 1980s. For example, premarital intercourse is commonplace today, as is cohabitation. Recent surveys of adolescents indicate that there is a lifetime prevalence of premarital intercourse of 31 percent for white and 63 percent for black youths. These behaviors indicate more permissiveness today than in the past, which implies that because people are more sexually experienced when they enter marriage they will have higher expectations of sexual satisfaction from their marital partners. Sexual gratification alone is no longer a reason for getting married, as it once was.

Women seem to be adopting an attitude of increasing control over their own reproductive functions. This can be seen in terms of both the prevention and the termination of pregnancy. For example, 64.9 percent of all married white women between the ages of 15 and 44 used some form of contraception in 1965, whereas by 1976 this had increased to 68.7 percent. By way of contrast, only 57.2 percent of married black women between the ages of 15 and 44 used contraception in 1965, and 58.5 percent used it in 1976. In 1973, there were 744,600 legal abortions, and in 1978 this number had almost doubled to 1,409,600. Another way of expressing this number is in terms of the abortion rate per thousand women. In 1972, this rate was 11.9 for white women and 21.9 for black women; the rates increased by 1978 to 22.7 for white women and 60.4 for black women (13).

Cohabitation has become increasingly accepted in the United States. It is very difficult to determine accurately the number of individuals who are cohabitating, since people frequently live together for relatively short periods of time, and these arrangements may never be formally reported. However, Glick and Spanier (22) have estimated that approximately 2.3 percent of all man-woman couples living together in the same household in

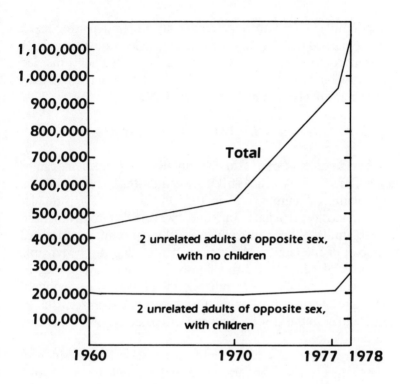

Figure 8. Unmarried couples living together in the United States, 1960–1978.

From Glick PC, Norton AJ: Marrying, divorcing, and living together in the U.S. today. Population Bulletin 32:5, 1977 (23), and U.S. Bureau of the Census, unpublished current population survey data for June 1975.

1978 were not married, representing a total of 1.1 million couples. Figure 8 portrays this dramatic increase in cohabitation. Furthermore, more than half of the people cohabitating have been married, usually reside in large metropolitan areas, and generally are characterized by having a relatively low income level and high unemployment. Although the majority of cohabitating couples are white, blacks contribute a disproportionately large share to the total numbers. Forty-three percent of all couples reporting had a never-married man living with a never-married woman, while 21 percent consisted of a divorced person living with a never-married person. Cohabitating partners that included a never-married man were most likely both college educated (22).

Contemporary Living Arrangements

The diversity of marital and family living arrangements can be seen from Table 9, which strikingly demonstrates that there is no one dominant family form in the United States. Of particular importance is the relative infrequency of single-breadwinner nuclear families (13 percent), which usually represents our idealized concept of the family. Many of our family and psychodynamic theories take for granted this family form and may, in fact, be somewhat inapplicable to other kinds of family composition. Dual-breadwinner nuclear families constitute 16 percent of all households in the United States and will in all probability increase in prevalence.

Today, the most prevalent form of household composition in the United States is the category in which people live in a child-free or postchildrearing marriage (23 percent), followed by the category of single, widowed, separated, or divorced persons, constituting 21 percent of all households. Surprisingly, 16 percent of

Table 9. Distribution of Adults in American Households

Place in Household	%
Heading single-parent families	16
Other single, widowed, separated, or divorced persons	21
Living in childfree or postchildrearing marriages	23
Living in dual-breadwinner nuclear families	16
Living in single-breadwinner nuclear families	13
Living in no-breadwinner nuclear families	1
Living in extended families	6
Living in experimental families or cohabiting	4
Total	100

From Ramey J: Experimental family forms: the family of the future. Marriage and Family Review 1:1, 1978 (24). Originally published by the U.S. Bureau of Labor, March 1977.

all households consist of single-parent families. These household prevalence estimates underscore the importance to clinicians of defining the particular kind of family under consideration, and they render such concepts as the family obsolete. These considerations are of particular relevance to psychiatrists concerned with family functioning. In particular, psychodynamic and child developmental theories must take into account the specifics of family composition.

Impact of Dual-Career Marriages and Working Women

The related phenomena of working women and dual careers in a family are subjects of much contemporary marital and family research. The Louis Harris Organization conducted an extensive survey of more than 1,200 people from the baby-boom generation, mostly individuals of middle and upper-middle incomes (25). In this sample, 95 percent were married and employed, and only a small proportion (less than 10 percent) maintained a single-breadwinner family arrangement. The majority of both men and women reported sharing of homemaking responsibilities, shopping for major household items, and joint decision-making about money. Almost half the men reported that they were cooking on a regular basis.

A second national study in this general area is the General Mills study, "Families at Work," which included more than 1,500 interviews of adult family members and almost 250 interviews of teenage family members (26). The adults in the General Mills survey were somewhat mixed in regard to their overall assessment of the circumstances in which both men and women were working outside of the home. About 52 percent felt that overall the dual-career arrangement had a negative effect on the family. The remaining 48 percent felt that the impact had been either positive or had no effect at all upon the general outlook for families. This sample also reported some thought-provoking findings in regard to children and their care within the current circumstances. It was indicated that almost 60 percent in this sample believed that children in their own family were cared for on a daily basis mostly by the mother. However, almost 40 percent felt that both mother and father should share equally in day-to-day child interactions and care. Of those family members who had to provide for daily care of their children while working, 48 percent utilized other family members (for example, older children or grandparents); 23 percent paid for help inside their home (for example, an arrangement with a neighbor or sitter); and 19 percent utilized day-care centers. Nine percent of the children involved cared for themselves after school and before one or both parents returned home. (These are referred to as latch-key children.) Parents reported a strong feeling that children have to become more self-reliant and independent when both parents work. Other interesting attitudes were determined, particularly among teenage girls. Although it was noted that the majority of the teenagers in this survey tended to have fairly traditional views of parental roles, the vast majority of the teenage girls planned to continue the trend toward combining work and family responsibilities. This observation was true for teenagers with working parents as well as those with one parent at home all the time.

A 1976 publication of the U.S. Bureau of the Census that used 1974 and 1975 data found that 20 percent of children with two working parents were cared for by another relative, 22 percent were cared for by someone unrelated to them, either in their own home or in the other person's home, and only 4 percent went to a day-care center (20). In 1980, a *Newsweek* article estimated that there were almost two million latch-key children in the age range 7–13 years (27).

In an extensive review of the research regarding working women in marriage, Waite (28) found that for both men and women time management was one of the most critical matters they faced. On the whole, it seemed that the working-couple arrangement did not create remarkably different circumstances for the dual-career couple compared with the couple in which the man filled a traditional work role and the woman remained in a homemaker role; and studies of general marital satisfaction have found that working wives report greater happiness than those who act as full-time housewives. The studies reviewed by Waite did not indicate substantial differences in regard to marital conflict or greater reporting of strain or stress when comparing the traditional with the working couple. The general trend reported is that there is a greater sharing in regard to decision making and marital power in dual-career couples. Summarizing the studies regarding marital power, Waite commented that they "suggest that this issue is becoming obsolete in any case as traditional roles of husbands and wives are becoming more and more blurred, and influence in decision making within marriage is increasing for all women" (28).

THE CYCLE OF MARITAL ACTIVITY

Categories of marital status, such as singlehood, marriage, divorce, and widowhood, are frequently portrayed as discrete and stable. Although there may have been some truth to this view in the

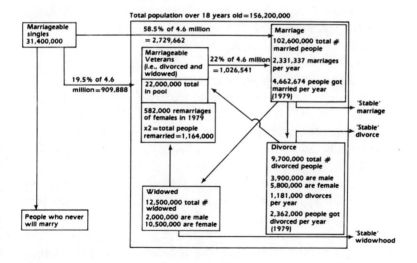

Figure 9. The Marital Cycle.

Reprinted from Bjorksten OJW, Stewart TJ: Contemporary trends in American marriage, in Marriage and Divorce: A Contemporary Perspective. Edited by Nadelson CC, Polonsky DC. New York, Guilford Press, 1984 (29). Reprinted by permission of Guilford Press.

past, it is no longer accurate. Rather, our review suggests a much more dynamic picture of marital activity in which large numbers of people shift between various marital statuses. Figure 9 depicts this flow of marital activity. It will be noted that we have used raw numbers of individuals in each marital status rather than percentages. Our reason for choosing this approach is that percentage figures are extremely difficult to interpret, since they depend entirely on which numerators and denominators are chosen, and they often do not provide an accurate portrayal of the baseline magnitudes of phenomena. The interested reader can calculate his or her own percentages using the raw data provided. As a good example of the difficulty just alluded to, most people know that our divorce rate is 49.2 percent in the United States today. This number is derived by dividing the number of divorces per year by the number of marriages per year and thus is not a rate in the epidemiological sense of the term, but rather a ratio between the magnitudes of two marital statuses. This ratio is fundamentally meaningless, since the frequency of marriage is not inherently or logically connected with the frequency of divorce.

Figure 10 depicts marriages by marriage order for the year 1979, and as can be seen, 55.5 percent of all marriages in that year were first marriages for both bride and groom while the remaining 41.5 percent of marriages involved at least one previously married person. Almost one fourth (22 percent) of all marriages were remarriages for both bride and groom. Eight to nine percent of marriageable adults never marry, a figure that has remained fairly stable over the past 50 years. Some researchers have predicted that a rise in the proportion of those who never marry will occur over the next 10 years. It will take a number of years, perhaps decades, to observe the long-term nature of this trend.

Although most Americans still marry prior to age 30, demographers and marital researchers have noted a general delay in marriage with more marriages occurring in the age range of 25–44. It is likely that the increasing educational level of women will continue to affect this delay to marriage. Marriages that occur at very early ages, particularly during the teenage years, are at much greater risk of divorce than are those that occur in later years.

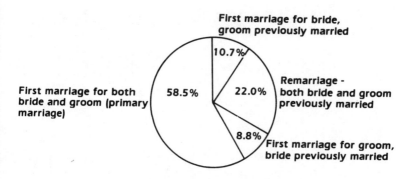

Figure 10. Marriages by marriage order.

From U.S. Dept. of Health and Human Services: First marriages: U.S., 1968–1976. Vital and Health Statistics Series 21(35):2, 1979 (30).

Teenage marriages, particularly for women, continue to be a major phenomenon (even with rising educational level of women noted above). Over the past 40 years, an average of 25 percent of all women were married by age 20. Teenage marriages are less frequent for men, since they tend to marry women younger than themselves, and the majority of men are usually in their early twenties when they first marry.

The extent of divorce activity in the United States is frequently referred to as an indicator of general decline in the importance of marriage and family living in the United States. Divorce has increased markedly in America in this century. However, it is important to appreciate several caveats and contextual matters prior to interpreting divorce data. As mentioned in our earlier discussion, although the divorce rate has increased markedly and the death rate has declined, they offset each other so that the total rate of marital dissolution has remained stable for well over 100 years. In other words, death and desertion have become less influential in marital dissolution, and legal arrangements through divorce have become much more of a factor. It should be remem-

Table 10. Divorces per 1,000 Population in Selected Countries by Year

Country	1910	1930	1940	1950	1960	1970	1976
United States	1.00	1.50	2.00	2.50	2.18	3.50	5.07
Canada	.05[a]	.08	.21	.40	.39	1.36	2.34
Mexico	[b]	.10	.22	.31	.43	.59	.27
England and Wales	.05	.09	.18	.69	.51	1.20	2.56
Norway	.20	.31	.32	.71	.66	.88	1.52
Sweden	.10	.36	.55	1.14	1.20	1.61	2.64
Denmark	.30	.65	.91	1.61	1.46	1.94	2.58
Finland	.10	.32	.36	.91	.82	1.79	2.14
Netherlands	.20	.36	.33	.64	.49	.79	1.52
Germany[c]	.30	.63	.92	2.47	1.34	1.61	2.67
Switzerland	.40	.67	.73	.90	.87	1.04	1.51
France	.30	.49	.28	.58	.66	.79	1.20
Japan	1.10	.79	.67	1.01	.74	.94	1.11

[a] Less than 0.5 thousand.
[b] Data not available.
[c] Rates for 1910 and 1930 for all Germany, later rates for East Germany only.
From Department of International Economic and Social Affairs: Demographic yearbook, issues 10, 20, and 30. New York, United Nations, 1960, 1970, and 1980 (31–33).

bered that there has been a general liberalization of divorce laws throughout this century which has contributed to the high divorce rates.

Table 10 indicates that although the United States has a divorce rate among the highest in the world, many other countries have experienced a much more rapid increase in their rates. For some countries, such as Canada, England, and Wales, the rate of increase has been especially rapid. The major point to be taken from this figure is that divorce has become a phenomenon of all developed societies, both Western and Eastern.

Another consideration beyond the international comparison is the matter of the utilization of divorce figures and data. Frequently, crude divorce rates based upon the total number of individuals in our population or total number of marriages are incomplete in portraying the marriage and divorce situation. As with most epidemiological data, a refined rate is a more sensitive and useful tool. Perhaps the most helpful divorce data are those derived from cohort studies that track the marital and divorce history of selected subpopulations. Table 11 provides cumulative percentages of divorces based upon cohort studies conducted by the U.S. Department of Health and Human Services. It can be seen in this table that for both first marriages and remarriages, by the time the fiftieth anniversary occurs for a couple, only slightly more than one half of the couples will still be married. Of interest is that remarried people seem to divorce sooner (that is, they don't put up with an unfortunate marriage as long) but with about the same

Table 11. Cumulative Percent Divorced by Marriage Order and Anniversary in the United States, 1975

Anniversary	First marriages	Remarriages
5th	16.3	23.6
10th	30.0	36.4
15th	37.4	42.7
25th	44.5	47.3
50th	47.3	48.9

From U.S. Dept. of Health and Human Services: National estimates of marital dissolution and survivorship. Vital Health and Statistics Series 21 (35):12,1979 (30).

frequency as people in first marriages. Thus, a remarriage has about the same probability of success as first marriages.

As with many other social phenomena, the differentials based on race and socioeconomic status are notable in divorce. The trend indicates that black individuals and those with a lower socioeconomic status are more likely to be divorced than are whites and those with a higher socioeconomic status.

A number of demographers are predicting a general decline or slowing in the increase of the divorce rate (34). Religious and legal as well as economic and time constraints on divorce have been reduced on a worldwide basis. It seems that the divorce gates have been opened, and a population backlog was released. It appears that once the logjam has been relieved somewhat, divorce rates will probably plateau or even decline.

As expected from the proportion of individuals having children and the great extent of divorce activity, children are very likely to experience the divorce of their parents. A concomitant to children's greater involvement in divorce is the substantial increase in the number and proportion of single-parent families and, with remarriage, stepfamilies and blended families. It has been estimated that stepfamilies make up 10 percent to 15 percent of all households in the United States, and a corresponding figure is that 10 percent of all children under 18 were living with both a natural parent and a stepparent (35, 36).

Perhaps the most profound change in regard to divorce is the effect that its general increase has had upon attitudes. In the past, divorce was viewed as at best a serious impropriety by a couple and at worst a moral or religious failure. Contemporary Americans seem to view it in a much more functional and personal manner. Graham Spanier described this set of attitudes about divorce and marriage in the following statement:

> Divorce is a response to an unsuccessful marriage relationship in which the spouses reject each other; they are usually not rejecting the idea of marriage or the family per se. Thus, divorce is not so much a statement about the viability of a married life or about family stability, but rather a realization of poor mate selection, lack of personal commitment, disenchantment with one's partner, or some other personal

or social problem surrounding a particular relationship. Persons approaching divorce usually report that they are no longer in love, that they have grown apart. (37)

Remarriage

Until recent decades, remarriage was primarily a phenomenon for widowed individuals. It is only since World War II that remarriage has become a more general phenomenon. As indicated earlier in Figure 10, 41.5 percent of all marriages in 1979 involved at least one partner who had been previously married. Reviewing 1980 data, Bjorksten and Stewart (29) reported that following a first divorce, almost 80 percent of the partners will remarry. Following a second divorce, almost 90 percent of the partners will remarry. Clearly, divorce does not seem to predispose individuals to post-divorce singlehood.

Of major interest in the remarriage picture is the effect of children on women's remarriage prospects. Table 12 indicates the relative probabilities of remarriage by a woman's age at divorce relative to the number of her children at divorce and years since the divorce. The presence of children is associated with an *increased* probability of remarriage for women in the age range 35–44 (although it should be pointed out that their children also are likely to be older and more independent). Although the presence of three children is associated with somewhat lower probabilities of remarriage as compared with childless women younger than 25, this difference is small. The table also shows that the median duration to remarriage for the women involved in the study reported by Koo and Suchindran ranged from 2.12 to 4.72 years.

In summary, a statement by sociologist Kingsley Davis provides an interesting interpretation of the relationship of remarriage to divorce:

> The significance of the brisk rate of remarriage is plain; it means that the American people do not have a high and rising rate of legal divorce and annulment because they're losing interest in marriage and a family. Rather, they have such a high rate because they desire a

Table 12. Cumulative Probabilities of Remarriage and Median Durations to Remarriage by Age at Divorce and Number of Children at Divorce (White Women Without Postmarital Births)

| | Women's Age (Years) at Divorce | | | | | | | | | | | |
| | <25 | | | 25–34 | | | 35–44 | | | 45+ | | |
Years since divorce	0	1–2	3+	0	1–2	3+	0	1–2	3+	0	1–2	3+
1	.2300	.2370	.2038	.1734	.2020	.1824	.0988	.1375	.0932	.0274	.0213	.0678
5	.7753	.7228	.6639	.5603	.5714	.5681	.2991	.3980	.3609	.1423	.2102	.2139
10	.9178	.8376	.7919	.7164	.7086	.7201	.3600	.5266	.5956	.2085	.2275	.3081
15	.9397	.8934	.8514	.7677	.7887	.7799	.4056	.5877	.7661	.ª	...	...
20	.9601	.9325	.9009	.8130	.8230	.8131	.4453	.6052	.8264	...	...	...
Median duration to remarriage[b]	2.12	2.20	2.65	2.61	2.73	2.49	3.68	3.04	4.72	...	...	...

[a] Insufficient number of cases.
[b] Life table median duration is the duration at which 50 percent of women had remarried, among those who had remarried in 20 years.

Reprinted from Koo HP, Suchindran CM: Effects of children on women's remarriage prospects. Journal of Family Issues 1(4):506, December 1980 (38). Reprinted by permission.

compatible and satisfactory family. Thus, despite a high legal divorce rate, a high proportion is married—higher than any other industrial society. Americans expect a great deal out of the state of wedlock and when a particular marriage proves unsatisfactory, they seek to dissolve it and try again. (6)

Figure 11 shows the remarriage rates for divorced and widowed people. Divorced men have the highest remarriage rate, followed by divorced women, widowed men, and finally widowed women. One reason for these relationships is that widowed people are usually older than divorced people and so may be less able to remarry, especially women, since men usually die before they do. Men seem to have more freedom to choose marital partners from a broader range of ages than women can, since men usually marry women younger than themselves. Thus, men may have more marital opportunities than women, leading to higher remarriage rates for both divorced men and widowers.

Clinical Implications

It is the purpose of this chapter to consider the impact that current demographic trends will have on the clinical psychiatrist in the future. Rather than deal with techniques of marital therapy, we will consider how the current social context may influence marital adjustment and pathology and the overall treatment situation. The clinical implications of current marital trends fall roughly into two categories: 1) our concepts of marital normality and reality and 2) the manifestations of marital problems.

Over the last generation or two, major changes in marital style have occurred from a traditional to a companionate pattern. Traditional marriages can be viewed from a structural perspective in which marital roles and duties were prescribed, nonnegotiable, and clear-cut. The focus of marriage was functional in that each partner was expected to fulfill role obligations. Marital failure was synonymous with role failure, which was easy to determine because there was good cultural agreement about what husbands and wives should do. These marital roles were closely associated with sex-role stereotypes so that men were reluctant to perform wom-

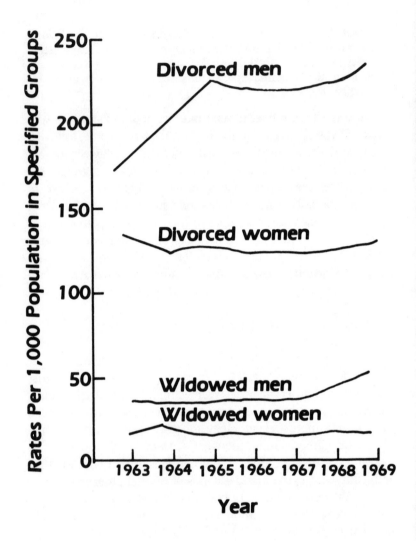

Figure 11. Remarriage rates of widowed and divorced men and women, marriage registration area, 1963–1969.

From Williams K, Kuhn RP: Remarriages. Vital and Health Statistics, Series 21(25):7, 1973 (39).

en's duties and vice versa. It was these sex-role stereotypes that connected marital role behavior with individual identity and thus related marital and individual pathology. These relationships justified the individually oriented psychotherapeutic approach to the treatment of marital problems.

The key concepts in traditional marriage were duty and responsibility. Duty implied a known set of role functions which one accepted upon marriage; if a person did not want to perform them, then he or she would not marry. Thus, in this sense, traditional marriage was binary. Once married, each partner was responsible for his or her role functions, that is, he or she was expected to perform them. If love occurred at all in traditional marriage, it grew after marriage and was by no means a requirement in the decision to marry; rather, one appraised a potential partner in terms of questions about his or her ability to perform role functions: Will he be a good provider? or Will she be a good mother?

The traditional marital style began to shift with the onset of industrialization in the latter part of the 19th century but did not really give way to the companionate style until the post–World War II era. The cultural upheaval of World War II and the postwar prosperity permitted reconsideration of marital roles in the context of the increasing status and freedom of women. It is beyond the scope of this section to consider the historical determinants of this shift of marital style, but most would agree that one of its main causes was the improvement in women's status.

The companionate style of marriage can be viewed from a process perspective, since it has an emotional focus in which roles evolve through negotiation and are often variable and vague. Communication and negotiation skills are vital in this style of marriage, and it is important that each partner have the maturity to know what he or she wants from the marriage. In contrast with roles in the traditional marriage, companionate marriage roles are created by the partners so that role competency is difficult to evaluate and marital failure is synonymous with poor relationship rather than role incompetency. Partners in traditional marriages must tolerate the stresses of adaptation to marital roles, whereas they must tolerate role ambiguity in the companionate form.

The key concepts in companionate marriage are love and choice. The raison d'être for these marriages is that people want to be together because they love each other and expect to obtain fulfillment from the relationship with the partner. The actualization of this romantic ideal is a historically new phenomenon that requires a level of prosperity sufficient to release people from a survival orientation and a degree of equality between partners hitherto unknown because of inadequate birth control, short life expectancy, and lack of economic opportunities and education for women. In short, the increased status of women has been a major factor in the rise of love, that is, companionate marriages.

The concept of marital choice implies not only choice within the marriage but also of the marriage. The freedom of both partners to choose to marry each other is a recent historical phenomenon and now appears to be an on-going matter after marriage, since divorce is relatively easy to obtain. We take for granted that women can leave marriage as easily as men, but this has only become possible in recent years when women have joined the work force and have achieved the economic freedom that makes this option possible. It may seem paradoxical that married people must continue to choose their relationship, since they have so much freedom to determine their roles within it, but along with choice and freedom come expectations.

The partners in companionate marriages have high expectations of each other and of the relationship. They expect to remain in love and to be happy. These expectations often lead to disappointment when romance settles into routine and the relationship is no longer exciting. This has led to the development of marital enrichment workshops designed to help partners achieve more fulfilling marriages.

In our consideration of marital normality, we must conclude that today there is a cultural mix between traditional and companionate marriage with the latter on the upswing and representing the cultural ideal of most young people. It must be recalled that the concept of choice within marriage is fundamentally companionate so that couples who choose a traditional style are in fact companionate.

The concept of the increasing status and freedom of women is not meant as a vague or philosophical term but rather as a description of demographic trends supported by many factors: increasing employment rates of women and increasing educational achievement (for example, more than 50 percent of college enrollments in 1980 were women); fewer children per woman; increased latency to childbearing; curtailed childbearing years; and increased utilization of day-care facilities, to name a few. With this increased status has come increased freedom of choice regarding intimate relationships. While this has permitted more love marriages, it has probably also contributed to a much higher divorce rate. Thus, the current marital reality is that marriage is much more tentative than it previously was, and women are much more able to decide the fate of their relationships.

Traditionally, the marital agenda usually focused on the development of a family (that is, children) and the acquisition of property (that is, a home). This agenda usually implied a high degree of stability so that roots could be established. Thus, psychiatric appraisal of marriage used these criteria, among others, to judge whether or not a marriage was working. Today, psychiatrists are faced with a much more difficult dilemma in evaluating companionate marriages. Since the focus is on love and the relationship itself rather than on children or property, the evaluation of marital success is based much more on the subjective appraisal by the partners than on external objective criteria. Couples may view their marriage as very successful, even though they have no children, move frequently (suggesting a rootless quality), and seem to the psychiatrist to be quite unstable.

It is important to consider our concept of normal marital stability, or the lack of it, in the light of the high rates of marital activity occurring today. It should be recalled that the median duration of marriage is 6.7 years, that more than one million divorces occur annually and that 80 percent of divorced people remarry. While it is tempting to say that this frequent change in marital status can lead to enormous levels of stress, it is probably also true that changing one's marital status is of much less significance today than it was in the past. It appears that although the immediate effects of changing marital status are probably still considerable, the long-term effects appear to be ameliorated by remarriage.

The currently high remarriage rate has several important clinical implications. First, it suggests that people are committed to the institution of marriage but may want to adjust it on an individual basis by changing partners. Second, attitudes about divorced people have changed in a direction of increased acceptance. Third, women are not disadvantaged in their remarriage prospects if they have children. In fact, the older a divorced woman with children is, the greater her remarriage prospects, that is, the absence of children seems to reduce older women's remarriage prospects. Fourth, the prevalence of divorce and remarriage suggests that these changes in marital status may be of less psychiatric significance than was previously thought. Finally, since on the average, one child is associated with each divorce, and most divorced people remarry, large numbers of reconstituted or blended families are being formed each year. This is one of the most important trends in our country today and will be considered in another chapter.

Current changes in marital patterns suggest that today there are large numbers of people who are living out marital styles that are substantially different from those they were exposed to as children. This leads to a potential conflict between what people were taught they should do and what they are actually doing. Since traditional marital patterns frequently have a strong moral or religious backing, these changes suggest that many people today are experiencing guilt about deviating from traditional norms. It appears that this marital guilt occurs primarily in today's transitional generation, since they are forced to reconcile their traditional marital socialization with the companionate marital reality. For example, some transitional generation men feel guilty when they don't perform traditional male marital role behaviors such as paying the bills or doing household repairs, while some women report feeling guilty when they don't do traditional women's work, even though both partners have agreed on role distribution. Although both partners may be clearly in favor of sexual role equality, their early traditional upbringing conflicts with their present behavior. This guilt can be very difficult for patients to understand, since they chose their marital roles and are aware that their behavior conflicts with their previous learning. The therapeutic dilemma of whether the patient should keep the guilt and change the behavior or keep the behavior and change the guilt can be very difficult to resolve.

This therapeutic dilemma leads us to return to our consideration of the changes in marital agenda and styles that have occurred over the last century. The traditional and companionate marital styles each suggest differences in marital pathology. In the structural (that is, traditional) model, since marital roles were prescribed and could not be easily changed, marital pathology was usually related to role adaptation.

Adaptational pathology usually took several forms. In the trapped wife syndrome, one of the best known forms of marital pathology, women were so constrained and bored by the repetitiveness and demands of childrearing and household duties that they became resentful, depressed, and angry and usually felt unfulfilled. One of the most common aspects of this syndrome was the increasing discrepancy between women's personal development and that of their partners. Thus, while the husband was experiencing new activities, job advancement, and external forms of personal validation, women were confined to endless chores which were experienced as increasingly meaningless. This characterization of the trapped wife syndrome is not to imply that all mothers and homemakers felt this way or to denigrate these marital activities. Rather, those women who experienced this problem usually reported these features as important. The most common clinical manifestation of the trapped wife syndrome was depression, for which many women sought psychiatric care. Since these women reported dissatisfaction with their marital role, psychiatrists often interpreted this as failure to adapt. Of significance is that as married women have increasingly joined the labor force, the prevalence of the trapped wife syndrome with its consequent depression has substantially diminished to be replaced by other kinds of difficulties.

Rebelliousness represents another form of role adaptation pathology. Some partners develop a negative or counterdependent identity characterized by a sense of self defined by defiance, that is, pushing against known or prescribed rules. This can best be seen in rebellious adolescents who define themselves by their disobedience. If this form of identity is perpetuated into adulthood, it can lead to difficulties in accepting a marital role. This is usually manifested either by people who blatantly break marital rules, for example, severe philanderers, or those who covertly cheat on their marital responsibilities, for example, people who gamble with the household finances.

Finally, role incompetence is another form of adaptational difficulty in which, for whatever reason, a person is incapable of performing his or her marital role functions. This can be caused by mental illness, inadequate preparation for the responsibilities of marriage, or many other factors. Thus, it made eminent sense for a traditional future father-in-law to be sure that his prospective son-in-law had a good job and seemed to be a competent person before the marriage took place.

Psychiatric treatment for role adaptation pathology usually took the form of individual psychotherapy aimed at helping the patient adapt. Treatment might be continued until the patient accepted his or her marital role or developed sufficient competence in it or both. This therapeutic concept had validity only as long as there was good cultural agreement about what constituted normal marital role behaviors for men and women. Thus, the answer to our therapeutic dilemma by those holding a traditional or structural view of marriage is to keep the guilt and change the behavior to be consistent with the traditional idea of a marriage.

In contrast with traditional marriages, companionate marriages, with their process orientation, lead to different kinds of problems. Since their focus is on emotional fulfillment, role functions are often not carefully considered during courtship so that marital difficulties may manifest themselves in terms of marital role definition and may include role ambiguity, power struggles, communication problems, and disappointed expectations.

Marital partners today are free to determine their own style of marriage, that is, determine who will do what in the relationship. On the one hand, this reduces much of the coercion that many partners experienced in traditional marriages, but on the other, it leads to problems in determining marital roles. Since partners are free to engage in a variety of marital roles, which ones they settle on depend on what they want and on their ability to negotiate. In early marriages, many partners are not sure which roles they really do want or should engage in. If they do decide, it is usually in a tentative fashion. This leads to a feeling of role ambiguity, that is, uncertainty about what to do in the marriage and how to do it. More importantly, many partners are unsure which of the following criteria to use to decide role behaviors: what they feel at the moment, what is "best," what their parents suggest, or what their friends are doing. This dilemma usually heightens the already present anxiety. Each partner may look to the other for help, but neither is really capable of helping, so both usually feel frustration, disappointment, and anger.

Since roles are not clearly defined in companionate marriage, each partner must fend for him or herself, which may lead to power struggles, that is, conflicts over which partner's preference will prevail. Negotiation requires a degree of maturity, tolerance, fairness, good faith, and clarity of one's own desires. Many partners develop a win-at-any-cost mentality which may be successful in the short-run but seldom works well in the long-run. They often develop the idea that losing a disagreement means their wishes will always be subjugated to their partner's. Gradually partners assume an adversarial stance and can no longer see themselves in the common endeavor of marriage. One of the earliest signs of this is when partners begin to keep a mental ledger of who won or of whose turn it is to give in.

It would be misleading to suggest that marital competition for power is new. Historically, in Teutonic marriages in the Middle Ages, each partner attempted to place his or her hand on top when asked to join hands during the marriage ceremony. Occasionally this led to such turmoil that the minister had to settle it, usually by putting the man's hand on top, thus symbolizing his supremacy in the marriage. In 14th-century France, laws were recorded requiring men to punish their wives for disobedience. Failure to do so was punished by making these husbands ride an ass backwards.

Although the struggle for marital power may have always occurred, in the past there was little doubt about who was right or wrong in the matter. Today, there is little consensus about who should be dominant, and most people advocate either equality (that is, symmetry) or parity (equivalent power but in different areas).

Communication problems are one of the most common manifestations of a variety of marital problems. They are usually the result of difficulties and in turn cause further ones, rather than the initial cause of problems. Communication difficulties are of particular importance in companionate marriage, since in many ways communication is the sine qua non of love and is required for role negotiation. It is difficult to imagine love without it. Thus, when communication begins to deteriorate, most people either view their marriage as becoming routine or as being problematic.

Companionate partners expect to feel love for their marital partners as well as receive it. When role definitional problems arise and partners feel frustrated and angry, their difficulties are often accentuated by their disappointment in not feeling love. Since marriage and love are equated, when other feelings interfere with love, the marriage itself is called into question, thus rendering companionate marriages very fragile during problematic times.

Role definitional problems in companionate marriage are best treated by conjoint therapy focusing on improving the relationship so that it is fulfilling for each partner. Treatment continues until partners are able to alter their relationship and/or interpersonal behaviors enough to be rewarding for each. While either partner may have his or her own difficulties requiring individual psychotherapy, the end point of the marital therapy is defined by both members of the couple. This will be described more fully in chapter 5. If conjoint therapy is unsuccessful some couples will divorce and try again. Therapists holding a companionate orientation would solve our therapeutic dilemma by choosing to have their patients keep the behavior and change the guilt, since our society has become less traditional in marital orientation.

Occasionally couples seem to have both kinds of role pathology.

They are usually old enough to have been socialized in a traditional mode but have had problems adapting to it. When their children leave home and they anticipate many postchildbearing years together, they may experience role definitional problems. While they have societal encouragement to develop the potential of their relationship, they may never have developed the communication and negotiation skills necessary to accomplish companionate goals. An educational approach to the marital therapy of these couples can be very helpful as can marital enrichment approaches.

As people live longer and must face more years in the postchildrearing era, role absence may come to be an increasingly important problem. By this is meant the situation in which people face many active years but are forced to retire from their jobs. The provider role for men is traditionally as important as the homemaker role is for women. When each of these roles is completed, people may be faced with a difficult adjustment period, well known to women as the empty-nest syndrome. Generally, this period heralds a positive time for women, but it also occurs much earlier than the role absence that men and women face upon retirement. Our society will need to solve this difficult problem as more people face this period of role absence which can lead to depression as well as marital adjustment difficulties.

One of the most important marital trends today is the aging of marital partners and their increased life expectancy. For the first time in history, people can expect to live for 20 to 30 years after their children have left the home. This means that people can anticipate two marriages in their lifetime: the first, a family-oriented marriage, and the second, a postchildrearing marriage. The criteria by which people may choose one kind of partner may be very different than those they use to choose the other. The increasing divorce rates among middle and older age groups suggests that these marital requirements may not always be compatible. The shift from one marital situation to the other occurs at midlife, thus making this transition of particular importance.

As partners live into old age, their children continue to grow and reproduce, leading to an increased prevalence of four-generation families. While this may sound positive, it also leads to the increasing economic dependency by the elderly on their children and grandchildren. The longer people live, the more retirement benefits they utilize, requiring more input by the active labor force. Examination of population trends by age suggests that there will be too many older people dependent on financial input by too few younger people. This problem is developing so quickly that some states are already beginning to examine children's incomes and to hold them responsible for their parents' welfare. Clearly, this will have an impact on family dynamics, but the form it will take is uncertain.

Specific Marital Trends

The cause-and-effect relationships between demographic trends and marital style can be difficult to determine. For example, are women working more because they are getting divorced, or are they getting divorced because they are working more? In all probability both statements are true to some extent, but there is no doubt that women are both increasingly divorced and employed. We will not attempt to determine causal relationships in the following discussion.

Increased Latency to Childbearing. Couples are deferring childbearing for longer periods than in the past. While this is associated with the companionate focus of marriage, it may also be related to women's increasing career focus and to the increased acceptance and utilization of effective contraception. Although childbearing is deferred, the vast majority of women still become mothers. This implies that women are gaining control of the timing of family events, which means that a woman's inability to do so may have a bigger psychological impact than in the past.

Fewer Children per Family. Whereas the average woman bore between five and six children in 1900, today she can expect to have between one and two. This decline has occurred not only because of contraceptive technology but also because women want fewer children. Children with few, if any, siblings can expect to receive a greater amount of parental attention than did children in the past. Maybe this smaller family size will be related to the prevalence of narcissism in the next generation.

Childcare. With millions of American women employed, alternative childrearing facilities have mushroomed. Thus, physicians concerned with childrearing issues may be forced to pay even more attention to the nature and quality of day-care facilities, not only with respect to the psychological health of the children but also with respect to epidemiological considerations.

Since child day-care is a relatively new phenomenon, many women experience some female sex role conflicts when considering utilization of day care. Some women feel guilty for "abandoning" their children to day-care because they view themselves as "bad mommies" for doing so. These feelings are frequently ameliorated as women receive more consensual validation from peers as well as "permission" from physicians. The dual-breadwinner lifestyle makes moving to a different city particularly troublesome, since both marital partners must begin new jobs, and nobody is left at home to establish the household. These couples are frequently dependent on established institutions for childcare, social interaction, and entertainment. It may be useful for the physician to become acquainted with these groups and advise new arrivals about them.

Encroachment on Family Time. The above considerations seem to suggest that there has been a significant diminution in the amount of time that families spend directly interacting with each other. Vast numbers of women are employed and thus spend less time with children. Families spend an enormous amount of time watching television and not directly interacting, and today many people feel that the most significant sources of gratification are external to the home. All of this leads to a pattern of family interaction characterized by decreased communication and negotiation and high degrees of fatigue. This is particularly significant in light of the increasing need for good negotiation skills by couples in companionate relationships. The implications of decreased interactive family time on children's upbringing cannot be overemphasized. As children spend more and more time watching television (the national average is six or seven hours daily), they will tend to identify more with role models portrayed on television than they will with the real live role models that their parents represent. As household technology improves in an effort to make the dual-breadwinner lifestyle more feasible, it leads to even fewer opportunities for family interaction. While it is difficult for the physician to intervene directly at the clinical level, we should pay careful attention to these trends at the sociological level.

High Divorce Rate.   While the psychological impact from divorce is diminishing compared with the past, it still represents a major stressor today. Divorce is usually accompanied by some social isolation and depression and is associated with increased morbidity and mortality. Since people seem to experience diminished physical resistance after divorce, it may be important for physicians to be especially vigilant for illnesses that are concomitant with immunosuppression, stress, and depression. While the depression associated with divorce is common and usually only requires reassurance, on occasion it can be severe and prolonged, requiring treatment with antidepressants or psychotherapy or both. The social isolation that most divorcing spouses experience usually requires little intervention with long-time residents of an area but may need to be addressed in more recent arrivals and may necessitate introduction of the patient into various organizations and institutions designed to facilitate the establishment of a social network. Many cities have group meetings of divorced people that may focus on the establishment of parenting networks or dating.

Since an average of one child is associated with each divorce, a need for custody arrangements is the norm. Divorce is becoming increasingly less adversarial today so that no-fault concepts of divorce are being applied to custody as well. Increasingly, joint custody arrangements are established and are frequently favored by courts. Probably the most important single factor in the success of coparenting is good communication between the members of the divorced couple. It seems paradoxical and thoroughly modern to suggest the idea that divorced people should communicate well, yet this is the case in the majority of couples that have joint custody of their children.

Legal Scrutiny. The high rates of marital activity in the United States suggest that people and families may enjoy substantially less privacy in the future and may be subjected to much more frequent public scrutiny of marital and parenting activities. Each change in marital status is accompanied by a legal process which usually has some aspect of regulation. For example, one cannot marry, or enter into any kind of contract, if one is legally incompetent. Divorce requires a legal process that demands that the divorce be justified, even if only on the grounds of mutual consent. If children are involved, custody arrangements are scrutinized by the court. The point is that changes in marital status represent access points for legal and public scrutiny of family life that are rarely present in stable marriages. Taken in this light, it should not be surprising that the courts have ruled on acceptable and even legal marital behaviors as in a recent case involving marital rape.

New Courtship Patterns and Agendas. The liberalization of sexual attitudes and behaviors hardly warrants comment today. However, the consequence of this liberalization is that fewer people marry for sexual reasons, and since most people are much more sexually experienced prior to marriage than in the past, they have much higher expectations for sexual satisfaction of both partners in marriage. This has both positive and negative aspects. Since fewer people are marrying for sexual reasons alone, the potential for marrying the "wrong" person diminishes. On the other hand, since expectations for sexual satisfaction are greater, there is significantly less tolerance for sexual dysfunction and an increasing demand for sexual therapy by physicians. Most older physicians are very aware that patients are much more forthright in sexual discussions, and it is important for physicians to educate themselves in sexual physiology and the treatment of dysfunctions.

Significant numbers of single Americans are now living with

partners of the opposite sex, which suggests that many people have a great deal of experience in quasi-marital relationships before marriage. This has led to a diminished tolerance for conflict and an increased awareness of what it is necessary to put up with in a relationship. Trial marriage is an ancient phenomenon and seems to have considerable value as both practice for marriage and as a new form of relationship. Not only are young people living together, but so are people in much older age groups including the widowed and aged, primarily for economic reasons.

The high divorce rate has led to large numbers of divorced parents who are interested in remarrying. Approximately 20 percent of these people will marry somebody who has never been previously married, and about 20 percent will marry another divorced person. Taken from the other point of view, approximately 40 percent of never-married individuals will marry somebody who has been previously married. While these phenomena are not new, their order of magnitude is, and this can lead to a number of consequences in the courtship situation. Divorced people who are dating each other are so accustomed to marital roles from their previous relationships that they frequently fall into a semimarital relationship too quickly. Because both partners know how to have a relationship, they enter into it without careful appraisal of the personal qualities of their potential partner. This leads to a greater likelihood that these individuals will be unhappily surprised when they finally pay attention to the personal qualities of their new partners. It is incumbent on the physician to warn divorced people of this tendency and to encourage them to slow down the progress of their new relationships and behave more like never-married individuals, that is, to make dates more specific and activity focused rather than relationship focused. The advantages of prior marital experience seem to be an increased awareness of what people don't like in their partners and a willingness to terminate new marital relationships that don't work well. When these relationships terminate, it appears that there is somewhat less stress involved. The overall odds of a second marriage ending in divorce are about the same as for a first marriage, but divorces occur more quickly in second marriages.

Large numbers of courting individuals today have children, which leads to a substantially more complex courtship agenda. Not only is the agenda to find a lover but also a suitable parent for the children. Needless to say, this can lead to confusion in making a decision about whether to marry. For example, if a woman finds a man to be an excellent and loving parent to her child, but not a particularly enthralling lover, she may tend to marry him anyway, thus leading to potential dissatisfaction later on as the children grow older. The potential for divorced men and women with children to marry too quickly is significant.

CONCLUSION

The physician must reconsider concepts of normality regarding marital and family patterns as well as realistic options for people who are considering changes in marital status. Physicians must become quite active with their patients during the courtship process and emphasize the need for flexibility and adaptability in a relationship, as well as the need to develop communication and negotiation skills. Parent-child interactions, especially in blended families, are enormously complex and little studied. It is premature to develop valid guidelines regarding these relationships, yet this will be a significant area of concern over the next 10–20 years.

The focus on companionate relationships, as opposed to traditional ones, will undoubtedly lead to a diminution of prevalence of the trapped-wife syndrome with its consequent depression but will also lead to an increase in anxiety related to role ambiguity as well as anger secondary to relationship conflicts. As people become more used to changing their marital status, stress accompanying these changes will probably diminish.

The myth of the extended family of bygone times may actually be realized by the vast network of blended families being formed in the United States today as well as the increased prevalence of four-generation families. These blended family networks represent a major homogenizing force whose major impact will be experienced not by the adults alive today but rather by the next generation of children. This will, in all probability, lead to a continuing decrease in the adversarial view of divorce and an increase in joint custody arrangements.

Marital trends and customs shift over time. The picture painted in this chapter must be viewed as a cross-sectional slice of American attitudes and behaviors in the 1980s. It is clear that Americans are interested in getting married and having children although they marry somewhat later and have fewer children. The high remarriage rate suggests that the institution of marriage per se is vital although individuals' tolerance for unfortunate relationships is significantly diminishing. The enormous backlog of unhappy people seeking divorce seems to be diminishing, and it appears that the divorce rate has peaked and is in fact diminishing slightly.

Americans are people accustomed to mobility and change, thus the high degree of marital activity is probably something that will remain in our society for some time to come. While this high marital activity may produce significant short-term adaptational stress, it may also help ameliorate marital depression and possibly even marital violence. Today people feel less trapped by marriage than ever before but, by the same token, more uncertain and anxious about their family institutions. Psychiatrists will be called upon to deal with this changing picture of marital problems.

References

1. Murstein B: Love, Sex and Marriage Through the Ages. New York, Springer, 1974

2. Laslett P: Social development and aging, in Handbook of Aging and the Social Sciences. Edited by Beinstock R, Shanas E. New York, Van Nostrand Reinhold Co, 1976

3. Shorter E: The Making of the Modern Family. New York, Basic Books, 1977

4. Demos J: The American family in past time, in Family in Transition, 2nd edition. Edited by Skolnick A, Skolnick J. Boston, Little, Brown, and Co, 1977

5. US Bureau of the Census: Current Population Reports. Washington, DC, US Government Printing Office, 1940, 1950, 1960, 1970

6. Davis K: The American family in relation to demographic change, in Demographic and Social Aspects of Population Growth, vol 1. Edited by Westoff CF, Parke R. Washington, DC, US Government Printing Office, 1972

7. Gordon M: The American Family: Past, Present and Future. New York, Random House, 1978

8. Metropolitan Life Insurance Co: Statistical Bulletin 65, July–September 1984

9. Rice DP: Projection and analysis of health status trends. Paper presented at the 106th Annual Meeting of the American Public Health Association, Los Angeles, October 1978

10. Kranczer S: United States population overlook. Statistical Bulletin 65:19, 1984

11. US Statistical Report, 1980

12. US Bureau of the Census: Statistical Bulletin 65:10, 1984

13. Cleveland WP, Gianturco DT: Remarriage probability after widowhood: a retrospective method. J Gerontol 31:99–103, 1976

14. Sussman M: The family life of older people, in Handbook of Aging and the Social Sciences. Edited by Beinstock RH, Shanas E. New York, Van Nostrand Reinhold Co, 1976

15. Statistical Abstracts, 1981, Table 46

16. Brody E: The aging of the family. Annals of Political and Social Sciences 438:13–27, 1978

17. Helsing KJ, Szklo M, Comstock GW: Factors associated with mortality after widowhood. Am J Public Health 71:802–809, 1981

18. US Bureau of the Census: Historical Statistics of the United States. Washington, DC, US Government Printing Office, 1975

19. Melville K: Marriage and Family Today, 2nd edition. New York, Random House, 1980

20. US Bureau of the Census: Current Population Reports. Series P-20, no. 358. Washington, DC, US Government Printing Office, 1980

21. Bane MJ: Here to Stay. New York, Basic Books, 1978

22. Glick P, Spanier G: Married and unmarried cohabitation in the United States. Journal of Marriage and the Family 42:19–30, 1980

23. Glick P, Norton A: Marrying, divorcing, and living together in the US today. Population Bulletin, 1977

24. Ramey J: Experimental family forms: the family of the future. Marriage and Family Review 1:1–7, 1978

25. House and Garden Louis Harris Study: How the Baby Boom Generation Is Living. New York, Conde Nast, 1981

26. General Mills American Family Report, 1980–81: Families at Work. New York, Louis Harris Association, 1981

27. The superwoman squeeze. Newsweek, May 19, 1980

28. Waite L: Women at Work. Population Reference Bureau 36:1–44, 1981

29. Bjorksten O, Stewart T: Contemporary trends in American marriage, in Marriage and Divorce: A Contemporary Perspective. Edited by Nadelson C, Polonsky D. New York, Guilford Press, 1984

30. US Department of Health and Human Services: Vital and Health Statistics, series 21, no 35. Washington, DC, US Government Printing Office, 1979

31. Department of International Economic and Social Affairs: Demographic Yearbook, issue 10. New York, United Nations, 1960

32. Department of International Economic and Social Affairs: Demographic Yearbook, issue 20. New York, United Nations, 1970

33. Department of International Economic and Social Affairs: Demographic Yearbook, issue 30. New York, United Nations, 1980

34. Glick P: A demographic look at the American family, in Family in Transition, 2nd edition. Boston, Little, Brown and Co, 1977

35. Espinoza R, Newman Y: Step-parenting. Publication no. (ADM) 78-579. Washington DC, US Government Printing Office, 1979

36. Glick P: Remarriage: some recent changes and variations. Journal of Family Issues 1:455-469, 1980

37. Spanier G: The changing profile of the American family. J Fam Pract 13:61-69, 1981

38. Koo HP, Suchindron CM: Effects of children on women's remarriage prospects. Journal of Family Issues 1:497-575, 1980

39. Williams K, Kuhn RP: Remarriages. US Department of Health and Human Services. Vital and Health Statistics, series 21, no. 25. Washington DC, US Government Printing Office, 1973

2

Marital Status and Psychiatric Morbidity

R. Taylor Segraves, M.D., Ph.D.

2

Marital Status and Psychiatric Morbidity

Clinical psychiatry has long suspected that interpersonal factors may influence psychological function and that dysfunctional interpersonal interactions may exacerbate preexisting psychiatric disease or even precipitate psychological difficulty in otherwise psychologically healthy individuals. However, there has been a relative lack of interest concerning marital relationships as a possible etiological factor in the pathogenesis of psychiatric disease, and training in family and marital therapy has often received a low priority in psychiatric residency training programs (1, 2).

The major purpose of this chapter is to examine the relationship of marital status to psychiatric morbidity. In the literature review that follows, a consistent pattern will emerge in which divorced and separated individuals are overrepresented relative to other marital status groups in terms of their admission rates to psychiatric hospitals and outpatient clinics. This consistent finding of strong relationships between divorced marital status and mental health service utilization has been subject to varying interpretations. One viewpoint, which tends to be favored by biologically oriented psychiatrists, regards both an unsatisfactory marital career and the onset of psychiatric illness as reflective of individual psychopathology in one or both spouses. This viewpoint (known as the selection or premarital disability hypothesis) suggests that mental disorder influences the attainment of different marital states. In other words, individuals with preexisting psychiatric impairment would have greater difficulty becoming and staying married. Their psychological difficulties would make them less attractive as potential mates, and the emotional turmoil associated with psychiatric illness would contribute to marital discord, separation, and divorce. An alternative viewpoint is to consider the relationship between divorced marital status and mental service utilization as reflecting both the protective effect that intimate social relationships have on mental health and the extreme psychosocial stress associated with marital disruption (3, 4). This viewpoint is known as the causation or postmarital disability hypothesis.

Each hypothesis would mandate a different form of response from the psychiatric community. If the premarital disability hypothesis is correct, the current relative lack of interest in marital therapy would appear justified. If, however, the postmarital disability hypotheses are correct, the psychiatric community might choose to allocate more resources to marital therapy and the alleviation of stress associated with separation and divorce.

METHODOLOGICAL ISSUES

To help the reader appreciate the significance of the studies to be reviewed, some of the methodological problems involved in obtaining and interpreting data concerning psychiatric utilization by different marital status groups will be briefly reviewed.

Basic epidemiological research is concerned with at least two types of information: the incidence and prevalence of a given disease. Incidence refers to the frequency with which new cases of the disease occur, and prevalence refers to the extent to which the population at risk suffers from the disease. The incidence of a given mental disorder can be approximated by first admission rates (for example, the annual number of first admissions for a diagnostic entity in relationship to the population of the catchment area served by that facility). Prevalence can be estimated by the resident patient rate (for example, the count of patients resident in a mental facility at a given time relative to the proportion served by that facility) (1). These rates can be used to provide measures of the relative differences in incidence and prevalence of specific disorders among different demographic subgroups. However, a number of other factors, including social, administrative, and economic issues, also influence admission to psychiatric facilities (5). There are difficulties in obtaining reliable data on the use of psychiatric services by various marital status groups. Different facilities utilize different methods for classifying and recording data. Some facilities report discharge rates rather than admission rates, and the Veterans Administration hospitals don't separate first admissions from readmissions. Many centers report marital status as married, widowed, never married, or divorced and do not separately index separated as a marital status subgroup. This omission may be a major problem as the period of greatest psychological distress may occur during the period of separation which often precedes divorce by one or two years (6). It is doubtful that reliable information is available on separated individuals. In census data, more females than males report their marital status as separated, suggesting the possibility of purposeful distortion of data by some respondents (7).

Although the National Institute of Mental Health requests data from psychiatric facilities about populations served, the reporting system is voluntary. Information from the private sector and from general hospitals that admit psychiatric patients is frequently incomplete. Information concerning the utilization of private ambulatory psychiatry care is obviously nearly impossible to obtain.

INDICATORS OF PSYCHIATRIC MORBIDITY

Marital Status and Psychiatric Hospitalization

Both prevalence and incidence data indicate that married individuals have the lowest rates of mental hospital usage of all of the marital status subgroups (1, 7). Most studies of institutional residence rates by marital status have found the highest rates in the never married, followed by the divorced and separated, widowed, and married, in that order (8). This finding is in keeping with the clinical impression that socially isolated chronic psychotics seldom become married and are often chronically institutionalized. However, studies of the incidence of mental disorder as determined by hospital admission rates, present a different picture. In these studies, hospital admission rates are generally highest for divorced and separated individuals, intermediate for widowed and single, and lowest for married individuals (9, 10). The finding of highest admission rates for divorced and separated individuals has been replicated in numerous studies in the United States and abroad. National surveys of psychiatric admissions by marital status have repeatedly found that divorced and separated individuals have the highest admission rates of any marital status group (11–17).

In many of these studies, the admission rates for the divorced were approximately 10 times greater than the rate for married individuals. Studies of admission rates in individual states and counties have produced similar findings. These studies have been consistent in finding the highest admission rates among the divorced and separated (18–23). Several surveys in foreign countries have reported similar findings (24–26).

Marital Status and Outpatient Psychiatric Service Utilization

As previously mentioned, it is difficult to obtain complete information on utilization of outpatient psychiatric services. Most of the available information concerns utilization of services in outpatient clinics and does not cover provision of outpatient services by individual mental health practitioners in private practice. Another problem is that all clinics do not report utilization statistics by marital status. The available evidence suggests that the divorced and separated are overrepresented relative to their proportions in the general population as users of ambulatory mental health services. In general, the age-adjusted admission rates to ambulatory psychiatric services for the divorced and separated are found to be highest of all marital status groups and approximately five times as high as comparable rates for married individuals. This finding has been replicated in national surveys at different time periods (27–32) and in surveys by independent clinics (33), surveys by discrete localities (34), and surveys in foreign countries (35, 36). In most studies the ordering of outpatient admissions by marital status parallels the findings for inpatient admissions. In other words, admission rates are highest for the divorced and separated, intermediate for the widowed and never married, and lowest for the married.

Marital Status and Usage of Nonpsychiatric Medical Services

It is well known that many individuals utilize general practitioners rather than mental health specialists in times of emotional crisis (37). Reliable information on psychiatric services provided by primary physicians is difficult to obtain; however, several well-conducted studies suggest that the divorced and separated are also overrepresented relative to other marital status groups as utilizers of medical services by nonpsychiatric physicians. Locke and associates (38) surveyed patient utilization of medical services from primary physicians in Prince Georges County, Maryland, in 1964. The physicians in the survey were asked to provide information on patients having psychiatric conditions. Highest rates of psychiatric conditions were observed for the divorced, separated, and widowed. A similar study was reported for patient visits to general practitioners in London, England (39, 40). Practitioners recorded every eighth consultation over a one-year period and diagnosed psychiatric conditions when present. The divorced and separated had the highest frequency of psychiatric problems of any marital status group. In a more recent study (41), utilization of medical services by participants in a health maintenance organization were studied. There was a marked increase in the utilization of health services evident in the six months prior to separation and continuing in the year following. The divorced and separated had significantly more health plan contacts during the two-year study than the married. The increased use of health-plan services by the divorced and separated appeared mainly due to their increased use of mental health services.

Population Surveys of Psychiatric Impairment by Marital Status

From the data presented up to this point, one can safely assume that the divorced and separated are more frequent users of psychiatric inpatient and outpatient services than any other marital status group. This group also appears to use general medical services for psychological difficulties more frequently than any other marital status group. Although the divorced and separated clearly utilize psychiatric services more than any other group, one cannot conclude that this group has greater psychiatric impairment than the married. In other words, data on service utilization are not necessarily reflective of the prevalence or the incidence of disorder in the general population.

Fortunately, there have been several well-conducted population surveys that have reported the prevalence of mental disorder in the general population by marital status. A variety of assessment procedures have been utilized, and the data have been consistent. Again, the divorced and separated have been found to have the greatest psychiatric impairment, and married individuals the least. Singles and the widowed have intermediate positions. In the Midtown Manhattan study (42), data were obtained from a stratified probability sample of Midtown residents by trained interviewers, and each member of the sample was then rated by psychiatrists for degree of psychiatric impairment. For both sexes, divorced individuals had the greatest incidence of psychiatric impairment. Several other interview studies have replicated this finding of the divorced group having the greatest impairment (43–46). It is also of note that two studies of the elderly have reported greatest psychiatric impairment among the divorced elderly. The divorced have been found to have even greater psychiatric morbidity than the widowed (47, 48). Population studies utilizing standardized questionnaires instead of psychiatric interviews have reported similar findings. The divorced have reported the highest degree of psychiatric symptoms of any marital status group (49, 50). Studies by the National Opinion Research Center have also reported that personal happiness is highest among the married and lowest among the separated, divorced, and widowed (51, 52).

Alcoholism, Suicide, and Marital Status

Both alcoholism and suicide are problems of psychiatric relevance which are frequently separately indexed. In both instances, the divorced and separated have higher rates than the married. It is clear that alcohol-related problems as indexed by alcohol-related hospital admissions (19, 53–56), deaths from cirrhosis of the liver (57), police arrest records (58), or positive results of breathalyzer tests in the emergency room (59), are most common among the divorced and separated. This finding is true for both males and females, although alcoholism is much more common among males.

There have been numerous national surveys of successful suicides by marital status in the United States. In general, these studies concur in finding the highest suicide rates among the divorced and widowed of both sexes (60, 61).

Most studies have reported the highest suicide rates among the widowed, followed closely by the divorced. Both groups have much higher suicide rates than the single and married (5, 7, 57).

In other countries, surveys have found suicide rates to be highest among the divorced, and the next highest among the widowed (5). Current data also clearly indicate that the divorced are overrepresented among suicide attempts (62–65). This finding has been replicated in the United States as well as in other countries. It is also of note that marital turmoil appears to be one of the major precipitants of suicide gestures (63–66).

Marital Discord and Psychiatric Impairment

It is clear that the divorced and maritally separated are greatly overrepresented relative to their proportion in the general population as users of mental health services. Similarly, population surveys have indicated increased psychiatric impairment in the divorced independent of help-seeking behavior. Clearly, marital status is a formal judicial arrangement and not necessarily always reflective of the quality of the interpersonal relationship. There is minimal evidence concerning the relationship of marital adjustment to psychopathology. One recent study by Renne (67) suggests that marital adjustment may be more closely related to psychopathology than to marital status. She studied a probability sample of households in Alameda County, California; participants completed questionnaires concerning their marriages, individual psychological health, and general health. Her data replicated previous findings of poorer psychiatric functioning in the divorced than in other marriage groups. However, when the data were reexamined using information concerning marital adjustment, she found that the relationship between mental health and marital status was only true for the happily married. On most indices, the unhappily married were equivalent in degree of psychiatric impairment to the divorced. Her study suggests that previous studies of the relationship of marital status to psychopathology may have underestimated the association of psychopathology with the inability to form satisfactory close interpersonal ties.

EXPLANATORY HYPOTHESES

As outlined in an earlier part of this chapter, various hypotheses have been posited to explain the differences in psychiatric morbidity among marital status groups. The help-seeking hypothesis posits that the differences in utilization of psychiatric services are related to marital status differences in help-seeking behavior rather than to actual differences in psychiatric morbidity. The observation that population surveys of psychiatric impairment also indicate greatest impairment among the divorced and separated is convincing evidence that the differences in utilization of psychiatric services by different marital status groups are not simply related to differences in help-seeking behavior.

The remaining hypotheses include the premarital disability (selection) and postmarital disability (protection or stress) hypotheses. Clearly, neither of these two hypotheses is sufficient in itself to explain the complex relationships noted between marital status and psychiatric morbidity. The selection hypothesis, which tends to be favored by biologically oriented psychiatrists (68), postulates that psychiatrically impaired individuals have difficulty becoming and staying married and that this explains the relationship between marital status and mental health service usage.

The selection hypothesis adequately accounts for the high resident-patient rates (prevalence) among never-married persons. There is a large population of poor premorbid chronic psychotics who are socially handicapped, who become hospitalized at an early age, and who become institutionalized (69). The selection hypothesis has considerable difficulty accounting for the differential among marital status groups. Viewing marriageability as an index of mental health, the selection hypothesis would predict the never-married population to have greater psychiatric impairment than the divorced (who were at least healthy enough to pair transiently) and would predict the impairment of the widowed and the married to be comparable to one another and lower than that of the divorced and the single. As previously reviewed, studies of psychiatric hospitalization, outpatient psychiatric treatment, and population surveys are in agreement that the ordering of psychiatric morbidity by marital status is quite different. The observed degree of psychiatric morbidity by marital status is as follows: divorced and separated (most impaired), widowed and single (intermediate), and married (least impaired). The premarital disability hypothesis could argue that the high association between divorce and psychiatric difficulty is the result of the incipient nature of late-onset mental illness, that is, as the illness progresses, it leads first to divorce and later to contact with the health care system. However, little is known about the impact of psychiatric disorder on marriage. Some authors have reported that the onset of affective disorder leads to marital disruption (70); however, others have reported that mental disorder may strengthen a marital relationship rather than lead to divorce (71, 72).

Adler (22) interviewed a random sample of admissions to Arkansas State Hospital and attempted to determine the time of onset of mental illness as well as the admission date. His data provided little evidence to support the selection hypothesis. Malzberg (20) reported that the selection hypothesis could account for the higher admission rates of nonmarried persons with a diagnosis of dementia praecox (schizophrenia), but not for other diagnostic entities. Probably, the finding that is most destructive to the selection hypothesis is the observation that the widowed have morbidity greater than the married and perhaps similar to the never married. The widowed would perhaps be similar to the never married. The widowed would be assumed to be biologically and psychiatrically similar to the same-aged still married couples prior to spouse death. The remarriageability hypothesis has been advanced by selection theorists to explain the high incidence of mental disturbance among the widowed. This hypothesis states that the higher morbidity in widows and widowers is a survey artifact related to the fact that healthier widows and widowers tend to remarry sooner than their more impaired counterparts. Thus, in any time sample, more healthy widows than unhealthy widows would have remarried and would be counted as married. The unhealthy widows and widowers would have remained single, unable to remarry because of their impairments. Thus, a given study would falsely exaggerate the association between widowhood and psychiatric morbidity. This novel hypothesis appears unlikely, as remarriages have not been found to select the healthiest among the divorced (67). Similarly, the remarriageability hypothesis is insufficient to explain the high suicide rates among the widowed as suicide deaths tend to cluster around the time of bereavement (60).

The postmarital disability hypothesis includes variations of the protection and stress hypotheses. Clearly, these hypotheses overlap to a certain degree. The protection-support hypothesis posits that marriage protects against mental illness by the provision of clear role definitions and by the establishment of social and kinship networks. Similarly, married individuals experience less stress because of the emotional support they receive from spouses (73). The stress hypothesis states that divorce and widowhood are significant life stresses producing psychiatric morbidity because of the abrupt changes in social roles and social networks.

Several lines of evidence tend to support the postmarital disability hypothesis. It has repeatedly been found that married students are better adjusted than unmarried students (74, 75). This finding is true of both undergraduate and graduate students. As the student population consists primarily of singles, it is unlikely that the selection hypothesis is operative for this population. Coombs and Fawzy (73) extensively studied an entire medical school class in terms of school withdrawal, stress, and anxiety and clearly found higher stress levels for single rather than married students. As single students married during their medical school careers, their stress levels declined. The authors concluded that their data provided strong evidence for the protection hypothesis. "A more tenable explanation of the relationship between marital status and emotional stress is that marital partners provide emotional support for their mates and thereby reduce tension (the protection/support hypothesis). The interview data provide ample support for this view" (73). If the protective function of marriage is related to emotional support, one would suspect that marriages of good quality would provide better support than marriages of poor quality. Obviously, the report by Renne (67) suggests that marital quality rather than marital status per se is related more strongly to absence of psychopathology. Similarly, strong relationships have consistently been reported between marital discord and individual psychiatric impairment (76–82).

The available evidence suggests that the association between marital discord and psychopathology is related to interactional factors for individuals with nonpsychotic psychiatric disorders. Mate selection may be of more importance in more severe psychiatric disorder. Several studies of the relationship of neurotic personality traits existing before marriage and the subsequent development of marital discord have found that only 9 percent to 10 percent of the variance in marital adjustment can be predicted from preexisting personality disorders (83–86). Other studies have found the concordance of neurotic illness in married couples tends to increase in magnitude as the length of marriage increases (87–89) and tends to be related to the quantity of activities shared with the spouse (90). By their suggestion that qualitative aspects of marriage are related to nonpsychotic psychiatric morbidity, all of these studies indirectly support the support-protection hypothesis. It is also of note that Parker and Hadzi-Parlovic (91) recently studied women at high risk for developing depressive illness. They studied mother-bereaved women who had poor relationships with fathers and stepmothers. Depressive illness was quite common in this group of women. However, in married women, the presence of an affectionate husband tended to protect against depressive illness. "Data for the married sub-group suggested that an affectionate husband largely corrected any diathesis to greater depression exerted by uncaring parenting, while the protective effects of caring parenting on adult depressive experience were largely undone by marriage to an unaffectionate husband" (91).

The stress hypothesis posits that marital disruption constitutes a significant stressor and can produce or exacerbate preexisting psychiatric impairment. The psychiatric admission rate data clearly lend strong support to the stress hypothesis. Similarly, data indicating a clustering of psychiatric decompensation around the time of marital disruption tend to support this hypothesis. In an extensive review of the literature on marital disruption, Bloom and associates (3) concluded,

> Perhaps the most appropriate interpretation of the research and conceptualizations that have been reviewed is that an unequivocal association between marital disruption and physical and emotional disorder has been demonstrated and that this association likely includes at least two interdependent components: First, illness (physical or emotional) can precede and can help precipitate marital disruption; and second, marital disruption can serve to precipitate physical and psychiatric difficulties in some persons who might otherwise not have developed such problems.

CONCLUSION

The purpose of this chapter was to review the evidence linking marital status and marital discord to psychiatric morbidity and to examine these data from the vantage point of various explanatory models. The data reviewed clearly indicate that severe marital discord, separation, and divorce are related to emotional unrest, help-seeking behavior, and the utilization of mental health services. Whether marital discord and divorce are etiologically related to more severe psychiatric conditions such as affective disease and other psychotic disorders is less clear, although the admission data to psychiatric facilities are suggestive of such a relationship.

The available evidence does suggest that marital discord, separation, and divorce are frequent antecedent events for the utilization of mental health services. These data assume greater significance when one realizes that the divorce rate in the United States increased by 79 percent from 1970 to 1977 (92). In 1976, 2.5 percent of the U.S. population was personally affected by divorce (3). Although the rate of increase in divorce appears to have moderated in the 1980s, the current divorce level is well above the trend line that extends back through an entire century (93).

Current evidence does not permit definitive conclusions regarding the explanation for the strong relationships observed between marital status and psychiatric impairment, and the explanatory models considered in this chapter are obviously too simplistic to explain all of the observed relationships. An adequate explanatory model needs to address the interaction of constitutional and characterologic vulnerabilities with environmental stresses. In other words, it is likely that preexisting psychopathology may contribute to marital discord and separation, which then accentuate the original pathological process. However, the magnitude of the relationship between divorced marital status and psychiatric impairment is suggestive that the loss of an intimate relationship may also predispose certain otherwise healthy individuals to psychiatric morbidity and usage of mental health services. It appears that relationship disturbances among intimates is an especially potent stress.

Clearly, providers of mental health services need to be cognizant of the turmoil associated with severe marital discord and separation, and they need to have the skills to respond appropriately. In this regard, it is sobering to realize that only a minority of training programs in psychology, social work (94), and psychiatry (2) provide training in marital therapy.

References

1. Segraves RT: Marital Therapy: A Combined Psychodynamic-Behavior Approach. New York, Plenum Press, 1982

2. Martin PA, Lief HI: Resistance to innovation in psychiatric training as exemplified by marital therapy, in Psychiatry: Education and Image. Edited by Usdin G. New York, Brunner/Mazel, 1973

3. Bloom BL, Asher SJ, White SW: Marital disruption as a stressor: a review and analysis. Psychol Bull 85:856–894, 1978

4. Bloom BL, White SW, Asher SJ: Marital disruption as a stressful life event, in Divorce and Separation. Edited by Levinger G, Moles OC. New York, Basic Books, 1979

5. Kramer M, Pollack ES, Redick RW, et al: Mental Disorders/Suicide. Cambridge, Harvard University Press, 1972

6. Bloom BL, Hodges WF, Caldwell RA, et al: Marital separation: a community survey. Journal of Divorce 1:7–19, 1977

7. Carter H, Glick PC: Marriage and Divorce: A Social and Economic Study. Cambridge, Harvard University Press, 1976

8. Brooke EM: A Census of Patients in Psychiatric Beds 1963. Publication no. 116, Ministry of Health. London, Her Majesty's Stationery Office, 1967

9. Bachrach LL: Mental Health, Marital Status and Mental Disorder: An Analytic Review. Publication no. (ADM) 75-217. Washington, DC, US Government Printing Office, 1975

10. Bachrach LL: Marital Status and Age of Male Admissions with Diagnosed Alcohol Disorders to State and County Mental Hospitals in 1972. Statistical note 120, NIMH. Washington, DC, US Government Printing Office, 1975

11. Kramer M: Epidemiology, biostatistics, and mental health planning. Psychiatric Research Reports 22:1–63, 1967

12. Kramer M: Statistic of mental disorders in the United States: current status, some urgent needs and suggested solutions. Journal of the Royal Statistical Society 132: 353–397, 1969

13. Pugh TF, MacMahon B: Epidemiologic Findings in United States Mental Hospital Data. Boston, Little, Brown and Co, 1962

14. Bachrach LL: Marital Status of Discharges from Psychiatric Inpatient Units of General Hospitals, United States 1970–1971, I: Analysis by Age, Color and Sex. Statistical note 82, NIMH. Washington, DC, US Government Printing Office, 1973

15. Bachrach LL: Marital Status of Discharges from Psychiatric Inpatient Units of General Hospitals, United States 1970–1971, II: Analysis by Referral Source, Length of Stay and Primary Diagnosis. Statistical note 83, NIMH. Washington, DC, US Government Printing Office, 1973

16. Bachrach LL: Marital Status of Discharges from Psychiatric Inpatient Units of General Hospitals, United States 1970–1971, III: Analysis by Hospital Control. Statistical note 84, NIMH. Washington, DC, US Government Printing Office, 1973

17. Milazzo-Sayre L: Admission Rates to State and County Psychiatric Hospitals by Age, Sex, and Marital Status, United States 1975. Statistical Note 142, NIMH. Washington, DC, US Government Printing Office, 1977

18. Frumkin RM: Marital status and mental illness. Sociology and Social Research 39:237–239, 1955

19. Locke BZ, Kramer M, Pasamanick B: Alcoholic psychoses among first admissions to public mental hospitals in Ohio. Quarterly Journal of Studies on Alcohol 21:457–474, 1960

20. Malzberg B: Marital status and the incidence of mental disease. Int J Soc Psychiatry 10:19–26, 1964

21. Thomas DS, Locke BZ: Marital status, education and occupational differentials in mental disease. Milbank Memorial Fund Quarterly 41:145–160, 1963

22. Adler LM: The relationship of marital status to incidence of a recovery from mental illness. Social Forces 32:185–194, 1953

23. Klee GD, Spiro E, Bahn AK, et al: An ecological analysis of diagnosed mental illness in Baltimore. Psychiatric Research Reports 22:107–148, 1967

24. Odegard O: New data on marriage and mental disease: the incidence of psychosis in the widowed and the divorced. Journal of Mental Science 99:778–785, 1953

25. Krupinski J, Stroller A: Survey of institutionalized mental patients in Victoria, Australia, 1882 to 1959, I: admissions to and residents in mental hospitals. Med J Aust 49:269–276, 1962

26. Lavik NJ: Marital status in psychiatric patients. Acta Psychiatr Scand 65:15–28, 1982

27. Rosen BM, Bahn AK, Kramer M: Demographic and diagnostic characteristics of psychiatric clinic outpatients in the U.S.A., 1961. Am J Orthopsychiatry 34:455-568, 1964

28. Biometrics Branch, NIMH: Statistical tables. Demographic and psychiatric clinics in the United States. Special report 1961. Washington, DC, US Government Printing Office, 1963

29. Biometrics Branch, NIMH: Socio-economic Characteristics of Admissions to Outpatient Psychiatric Services, 1969. Publication no. (HSM) 72-9045. Washington, DC, US Government Printing Office, 1971

30. Meyer NG: Admissions to Outpatient Psychiatric Services by Age, Sex, Color, and Marital Status, June 1970–May 1971. Statistical note 79, NIMH. Washington, DC, US Government Printing Office, 1973

31. Redick RW, Johnson C: Marital Status, Living Arrangements and Family Characteristics of Admissions to State and County Mental Hospitals and Outpatient Psychiatric Clinics, United States, 1970. Statistical note 100, NIMH. Washington, DC, US Government Printing Office, 1974

32. Rosen BM, Anderson TE, Bahn AK: Psychiatric services for the aged: a nationwide survey of patterns of utilization. J Chron Dis 21:167–177, 1968

33. McKnight RS, Reznikoff M, Mulligan R, et al: Characteristics of patients in an adult outpatient clinic: a survey and evaluation. Am J Orthopsychiatry 36:636–642, 1966

34. Miles HC, Gardner EA, Bodian C, et al: A cumulative survey of all psychiatric experiences in Monroe County, New York. Psychiatr Q 38:458–487, 1964

35. Robertson NC: The relationship between marital status and the risk of psychiatric referral. Br J Psychiatry 124:191–202, 1974

36. Innes G, Sharp GA: A study of psychiatric patients in North-East Scotland. Journal of Mental Science 108:447–456, 1962

37. Gurin G, Veroff J, Feld S: Americans View Their Mental Health. New York, Basic Books, 1960

38. Locke BZ, Finucane DL, Hassler F: Emotionally disturbed patients under care of private non-psychiatric physicians. Psychiatric Research Reports 22:235–248, 1967

39. Shepherd M, Cooper B, Brown A, et al: Psychiatric Illness in General Practices. Oxford, Oxford University Press, 1966

40. Cooper B: Psychiatric disorder in hospital and general practice. Soc Psychiatry 1:7–10, 1966

41. Wertlieb D, Budman S, Demby A, et al: The stress of marital separation: intervention in a health maintenance organization. Psychosom Med 44:437–447, 1982

42. Srole L, Langner TS, Michael SD, et al: Mental Health in the Metropolis: The Midtown Manhattan Study. New York, McGraw-Hill, 1962

43. Briscoe CW, Smith JB, Robins E, et al: Divorce and psychiatric disease. Arch Gen Psychiatry 29:119–125, 1973

44. Briscoe CW, Smith JB: Psychiatric illness, marital units and divorce. J Nerv Men Dis 158: 440–445, 1974

45. Blumenthal MD: Mental health among divorced. Arch Gen Psychiatry 16:603–608, 1967

46. Pearlin LI, Johnson JS: Marital status, lifestrains and depression. American Sociological Review 42:704–715, 1977

47. Bellin SS, Hardt RM: Marital status and mental disorders among the aged. American Sociological Review 23:155–162, 1958

48. Lowenthal MF, Berkman PL, Brissette GG, et al: Aging and Mental Disorder, San Francisco. San Francisco, Jossey-Bass, 1967

49. Uhlenhuth EH, Lipman RS, Balter MB, et al: Symptom intensity and life stress in the city. Arch Gen Psychiatry 31:759–764, 1974

50. Mellinger GD, Blater MB, Manheimer DL, et al: Psychic distress, life crisis, and use of psychotherapeutic medications. Arch Gen Psychiatry 35:1045–1052, 1978

51. Bradburn NM: The Structure of Psychological Well-Being. Hawthorne, NY, Aldine, 1969

52. Bradburn NM, Caplovitz D: Reports on Happiness. Hawthorne, NY, Aldine, 1965

53. Gorwitz K, Bahn A, Warthen FJ, et al: Some epidemiological data on alcoholism in Maryland. Quarterly Journal of Studies on Alcohol 31:423–443, 1970

54. Malzberg B: A study of first admission with alcoholic psychosis in New York State, 1943–1944. Quarterly Journal of Studies on Alcohol 8:274–295, 1947

55. Rosenblatt SM, Gross MM, Chartoff S: Marital status and multiple psychiatric admission for alcoholism. Quarterly Journal of Studies on Alcohol 30:445–447, 1969

56. Rosenblatt SM, Gross MM, Malenowski B, et al: Marital status and multiple psychiatric admissions for alcoholism: a cross validation. Quarterly Journal of Studies on Alcohol 32:1092–1096, 1971

57. Gove WR: Sex, marital status, and mortality. American Journal of Sociology 79:45–67, 1973

58. Bacon SD: Inebriety, social integration and marriage. Quarterly Journal of Studies on Alcohol 5:86–125, 1944

59. Wechsler H, Thum D, Demone HW, et al: Social characteristics and blood alcohol. Quarterly Journal of Studies on Alcohol 23:132–147, 1972

60. Wenz FV: Marital status, anomie, and forms of social isolation: a case of high suicide rate among the widowed in an urban sub-area. Diseases of the Nervous System 38:891–895, 1977

61. Modan B, Nissenkorn I, Lewkowski SR: Comparative epidemiologic aspects of suicide and attempted suicide in Israel. Am J Epidemiol 91:393-399, 1970

62. Weissman MM: The epidemiology of suicide attempts, 1960 to 1971. Arch Gen Psychiatry 30:737-746, 1974

63. Kessel N: Self-poisoning, parts 1 and 2. Br Med J 2:1265–1270, 1336–1340, 1965

64. Smith JS, Davison K: Changes in the pattern of admissions for attempted suicide in Newcastle Upon Tyne during the 1960's. Br Med J 4:412–415, 1971

65. Edwards JE, Whitlock FA: Suicide and attempted suicide in Brisbane. Med J Aust 55:932–938, 1968

66. Sclare AD, Hamilton CM: Attempted suicide in Glasgow. Br J Psychiatry 109:609–615, 1963

67. Renne KS: Health and marital experience in an urban population. Journal of Marriage and the Family 33:338-350, 1971

68. Merkangas KR, Bromet EJ, Spiker DJ: Assortive mating, social adjustment, and course of illness in primary affective disorder. Arch Gen Psychiatry 40:795–800, 1983

69. Segraves RT: Marriage and mental health. J Sex Marital Ther 6:187–198, 1980

70. Lesser AL: Hypomania and marital conflict. Can J Psychiatry 28: 362–366, 1983

71. Clausen JA: The marital relationship antecedent to hospitalization of a spouse for mental illness. Presented at the Annual Meeting of the American Sociological Association, Chicago, September 1959

72. DuPont RL, Ryder RG, Grunebaum HU: An unexpected result of psychosis in marriage. Am J Psychiatry 128:735–739, 1971

73. Coombs RH, Fawzy FL: The effect of marital status on stress in medical school. Am J Psychiatry 1139:1490–1493, 1982

74. Busselen HJ, Busselen CK: Adjustment differences between married and single undergraduate university students: an historical perspective. FAM Coor, 24:281–287, 1975

75. Watson G: Happiness among adult students of education. J Educ Psychol 21:79–109, 1930

76. Dean DG: Emotional maturity and marital adjustment. Journal of Marriage and the Family 28:454–457, 1966

77. Murstein BI, Glaudin V: The use of the MMPI in the determination of marital adjustment. Journal of Marriage and the Family 30:651–655, 1968

78. Kelly EL: Marital compatibility as related to personality traits of husbands and wives as rated by self and spouse. J Soc Psychol 13:193–198, 1941

79. Barry WA: Marriage research and conflict: an integrative review. Psychol Bull 73:41–54, 1970

80. Burchinal LG, Hawkes GR, Gardner B: Personality characteristics and marital satisfaction. Social Forces 35:218–222, 1957

81. Karlsson G: Adaptability and Communication in Marriage: A Swedish Predictive Study of Marital Satisfaction. Uppsala, Almquist and Wiksell, 1951

82. Locke HJ, Karlsson G: Marital adjustment and prediction in Sweden and the United States. American Sociological Review 17:10–17, 1952

83. Kelly EL: Concerning the validity of Terman's weights for predicting marital happiness. Psychol Bull 139:202–203, 1939

84. Terman LM: Prediction data: predicting marriage failure from test scores. Marriage and Family Living 12:51–54, 1950

85. Adams CR: The prediction of adjustment in marriage. Educational and Psychological Measurements 6:185–193, 1946

86. Burgess EW, Wallin P: Engagement and Marriage. New York, JB Lippincott Co, 1953

87. Kreitman N: Mental disorder in married couples. Journal of Mental Science 108:438–446, 1962

88. Kreitman N: Married couples admitted to mental hospitals. Br J Psychiatry 114:669–718, 1968

89. Kreitman N, Collins J, Nelson B, et al: Neurosis and marital interaction, I. Personality and symptoms. Br J Psychiatry 117:33–46, 1970

90. Nelson B, Collins N, Kreitman N, et al: Neurosis and marital interaction, II: time sharing and social activity. Br J Psychiatry 117:47–58, 1970

91. Parker G, Hadzi-Pavlovic D: Modification of levels of depression in mother-bereaved women by parental and marital relationships. Psychol Medicine 14:125–135, 1984

92. US Bureau of the Census: Current Population Reports. Marital status and living arrangements, March 1977. Series P-20, no. 323 Washington, DC, US Government Printing Office, 1978

93. Glick PC: Marriage, divorce, and living arrangements. Journal of Family Issues 5:7–26, 1984

94. Prochaska J, Prochaska J: Twentieth century trends in marriage and marital therapy, in Marriage and Marital Therapy. Edited by Paoline TJ, McGrody BS. New York, Brunner/Mazel, 1978

3

Marital Status and Health

Oliver J. W. Bjorksten, M.D.
Thomas J. Stewart, Ph.D.

3

Marital Status and Health

It has been a long-standing epidemiological observation that in terms of physical and mental health, as well as mortality, marriage is "good for people," especially for men. This chapter reviews the available data and presents some hypotheses to explain the relationship between marital status and health. Coupled with Chapter 2, this one provides an overview of the clinical impact of marital status upon health and mental health.

MARRIAGE AND MORTALITY

The most pronounced difference among people of various marital statuses occurs in mortality figures. In almost every circumstance (even considering race, gender, and other modifying factors), the married have lower death rates than comparable unmarried people. This pattern has been evident since the 1930s when mortality data were first reported utilizing marital status as a variable. Figure 1 and Tables 1 and 2 are adapted from the Carter and Glick report, one of the most definitive analyses of marital status and health (1). (Unfortunately, data are not routinely categorized by marital status for death certificates and other sources. Special reports are periodically published using marital status as a major variable.) Figure 1 indicates that, by both race and gender, those who are

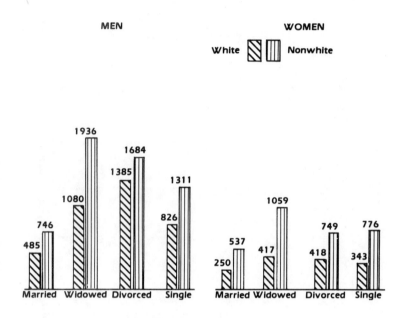

Figure 1. Death rate per 100,000 persons 15 to 64 years old by marital status,
standardized for age in the United States, 1959 to 1961.
From the National Center for Health Statistics, unpublished data.

married have lower death rates than those who are widowed,
divorced, or single. Among black men, the widowed and divorced
have death rates that are more than 150 percent and 100 percent
higher, respectively, than the married. The trends vary slightly for
white men: while the proportional differences are approximately
the same, divorced men have higher death rates than do the
widowed, followed by the married. In other words, married men
(be they black or white) have the lowest mortality, followed by
single men. The worst rates, dependent upon race, are for those
who are widowed or divorced.

The relative health advantages of married life seem to be more
pronounced for men than for women. Although the same trend is
evident for female death rates, the differences between married

Table 1. Average Annual Death Rates Per 100,000 Men Aged 15–64, From Selected Causes, by Marital Status and Color, Standardized for Age in the United States, 1959–1961

Cause of death	White men				Nonwhite men			
	Single	Married	Widowed	Divorced	Single	Married	Widowed	Divorced
Coronary disease and other myocardial (heart) degeneration	237	176	275	362	231	142	328	298
Motor-vehicle accidents	54	35	142	128	62	43	103	81
Cancer of respiratory system	32	28	43	65	44	29	56	75
Cancer of digestive organs	38	27	39	48	62	42	90	88
Vascular lesions (stroke)	42	24	46	58	105	73	176	132
Suicide	32	17	92	73	16	10	41	21
Cancer of lymph glands and of blood-making tissue	13	12	11	16	13	11	15	18
Cirrhosis of liver	31	11	48	79	40	12	39	53
Rheumatic fever (heart)	14	10	21	19	14	8	16	19
Hypertensive heart disease	16	8	16	20	68	49	106	90
Pneumonia	31	6	25	44	68	22	78	69
Diabetes mellitus	13	6	12	17	68	11	22	22
Homicide	7	4	16	30	79	51	152	129
Chronic nephritis	7	4	7	7	18	11	26	21
Accidental falls	12	4	11	23	19	7	23	19
Tuberculosis, all forms	17	3	18	30	50	15	62	54
Cancer of prostate gland	3	3	3	4	7	8	15	12
Accidental fire or explosion	6	2	18	16	15	5	24	16
Syphilis	2	1	2	4	10	6	14	15

Reprinted from Carter H, Glick P. Marriage and Divorce: A Social and Economic Study. Cambridge, Harvard University Press, 1970 (1). Copyright © 1970 by Harvard University Press. Reprinted by permission.

Table 2. Average Annual Death Rates per 100,000 Women Aged 15–64, From Selected Causes, by Marital Status and Color, Standardized for Age in the United States, 1959–1961

Cause of death	White women				Nonwhite women			
	Single	Married	Widowed	Divorced	Single	Married	Widowed	Divorced
Coronary disease and other myocardial (heart) degeneration	51	44	67	62	112	83	165	113
Cancer of breast	29	21	21	23	26	19	28	27
Cancer of digestive organs	24	20	24	23	33	25	41	35
Vascular lesions (stroke)	23	19	31	28	89	72	147	82
Motor-vehicle accidents	11	11	47	35	13	10	25	20
Rheumatic fever (heart)	14	10	15	13	14	8	12	13
Cancer of lymph glands and of blood-making tissue	9	8	9	8	7	7	9	13
Hypertensive heart disease	8	7	10	9	63	50	97	56
Cancer of cervix	4	7	13	18	22	17	34	27
Diabetes mellitus	7	7	11	8	24	20	36	22
Cirrhosis of liver	6	7	15	20	20	9	23	20
Cancer of ovary	12	7	8	8	8	6	9	8
Suicide	8	6	12	21	3	3	6	5
Cancer of respiratory system	5	5	6	7	6	5	9	10
Pneumonia	15	4	7	10	11	12	31	22
Chronic nephritis	4	3	5	4	14	11	16	11
Homicide	1	2	7	9	17	14	33	25
Tuberculosis, all forms	5	2	4	5	24	8	19	16
Accidental fire or explosion	2	1	6	4	6	4	11	5

Reprinted from Carter H, Glick P: Marriage and Divorce: A Social and Economic Study. Cambridge, Harvard University Press, 1970 (1). Copyright © 1970 by Harvard University Press. Reprinted by permission.

and nonmarried categories are not as marked as they are for men. For nonwhite men and women, the widowed stand out because they have the highest death rates.

Tables 1 and 2 outline the leading causes of death by marital status for men and women, as well as selected other causes that are of interest in an analysis of mortality and marital status. Table 1 indicates that, with only a few exceptions, married men consistently have the lowest death rates for the reported causes. The exceptions for white men are cancer of the lymph glands and cancer of the prostate. For nonwhite men the only exception is cancer of the prostate. Some of the differentials between married and nonmarried men are interesting; for example, the death rates from motor vehicle accidents are almost four times higher for widowed and divorced white men than married ones. Suicide rates for widowed and divorced white men are more than four and three times higher, respectively, than for married men; among black men death rates from cirrhosis of the liver are four times higher for divorced and three times higher for widowed than for married men. The table also reflects the differential between whites and nonwhites in regard to rates of death due to homicide, with nonwhite men having higher rates in all categories. However, it is noted that married black men have the lowest rate of death due to homicide among all black men.

The same general trends are evident for both white and nonwhite women, but the differences are not as dramatic. For the most part, married women have the lowest reported death rates for the majority of the causes included in the table.

It is notable that the widowed and divorced have high rates of accidental deaths involving motor vehicles, falls, fires, and explosions. This probably reflects in part a new set of circumstances that places widowed and divorced people at greater risk for accidents, since they probably drive more themselves and have to do more housework on their own. The never-married may be used to living on their own, which may contribute to their lower rates of death from accidents.

Figure 2 is another way of depicting the relative position of married white men relative to unmarried white men for malig-

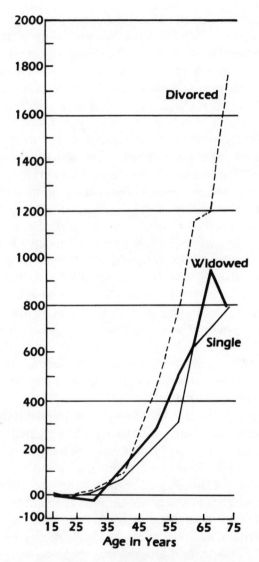

Figure 2. Excess risk of death per 100,000 population for malignant neoplasm of digestive organs and peritoneum in the unmarried white male population, by age in the United States, 1959–61.
From National Center for Health Statistics: Mortality from Selected Causes by Marital Status, Part A. Series 20, No. 8a. Washington, D.C., U.S. Government Printing Office, 1970 (2).

nant neoplasm of digestive organs and peritoneum. In this figure, the death rate per 100,000 population for white married men serves as the standard upon which the excess rates of the divorced, widowed, and single are calculated.

Another source of analysis for the 1959–1961 data on marital status and mortality was a special publication of the National Center for Health Statistics (2). This report found that white married men and women had in common four of the five leading causes of death: 1) coronary heart disease and other myocardial degeneration, 2) motor vehicle accidents, 3) cancer of the digestive system, and 4) vascular lesions. Taken together, these causes accounted for 54 percent of all deaths among white married men and 37 percent of all deaths among white married women (15–64 years of age). Nonwhite married men and women have in common three of four leading causes of death: 1) coronary disease and other myocardial degenerations, 2) vascular lesions (which they share in common with whites), and 3) hypertensive heart disease. Homicide was a leading cause of death for nonwhite men and diabetes for nonwhite women. These data also indicated that nonwhite husbands had high rates of death due to homicide, accidental falls, and fires or explosions, which accounted for eight percent of all their deaths compared with only two percent among their white counterparts.

Utilizing more recent data, Kobrin and Hendershot reported essentially the same patterns of mortality by marital status (3). Table 3 demonstrates that in all age groups married people have the most favorable death rates. Kobrin and Hendershot added a refinement to the analyses of marital status and mortality by adding the presence or absence of children as a variable (Table 4). They found that among the married, those who had children living with them, regardless of age, had lower death rates. Veevers' analysis of suicide rates confirmed that the presence of children seemed to have a beneficial effect on death rates (4).

Widowhood has been extensively studied from the 1950s to the present, and some researchers have even used longitudinal methods. Three early studies in Great Britain found that widows and widowers were at substantially greater risk for both death and

Table 3. Deaths per 100,000 by Age, According to Sex and Marital Status:
United States, 1966–1968

Marital status and sex	Age			
	35–44	45–54	55–64	65–74
Male				
Married	323	814	2,042	4,456
Nonmarried	1,008	2,125	4,276	5,944
Ratio[a]	3.12	2.61	2.09	1.33
Female				
Married	212	464	910	2,379
Nonmarried	408	757	1,278	2,595
Ratio[a]	1.92	1.63	1.40	1.09

[a] Nonmarried to married.

Reprinted from Kobrin FE, Hendershot GE: Do family ties reduce mortality: evidence from
the U.S., 1966–1968. Journal of Marriage and the Family 39:737–745, November 1977 (3).
Copyrighted 1977 by the National Council on Family Relations, 1910 West Country Road
B, Suite 147, St. Paul, Minnesota 55113. Reprinted by permission.

Table 4. Deaths per 100,000 by Age, According to Sex and Presence of
Children, Married Persons: United States, 1966–1968

Presence of children and sex	Age		
	35–44	45–54	55–64
Male			
Children under 18 present	268	695	2,118
Children under 18 absent	557	892	1,930
Ratio[a]	2.1	1.3	.9
Female			
Children under 18 present	160	331	777[b]
Children under 18 absent	378	523	567
Ratio[a]	2.4	1.6	1.1
Ratio of female and male ratios	1.1	1.2	1.2

[a] Absent to present.
[b] Fewer than 100 deaths.

Reprinted from Kobrin, FE, Hendershot GE: Do family ties reduce mortality: evidence from
the U.S., 1966–1968. Journal of Marriage and Family 39:737–745, November 1977 (3).
Copyrighted 1977 by the National Council on Family Relations, 1910 West Country Road
B, Suite 147, St. Paul, Minnesota 55113. Reprinted by permission.

illness than were married individuals (5–7) and that this risk was
highest for a brief period of time following the death of the spouse.

The most recent study of a cohort of widowed individuals in
Maryland indicated that this increase of mortality is greater for

men than for women (8). Additionally, Helsing et al. found that death rates among widowed men who remarried were much lower than among those who did not. This amelioration of the bereavement mortality was so striking that the author cautiously suggested that the widowed might be encouraged to remarry as a way of benefiting their health status.

MORBIDITY, HOSPITALIZATION, AND UTILIZATION OF MEDICAL CARE

We have already seen that marital disruption appears to have an adverse effect on death rates. We now turn to an examination of its impact on morbidity. It is very difficult to make an accurate estimate of illness rates in a population, since it is virtually impossible to measure the number of illness episodes for each individual. The most common approach to estimating morbidity is to measure the utilization rates of various health care indicators. Table 5, taken in part from an unpublished survey by Somers, presents summary data for the effect of marital status on five health care indicators, each of which represents an attempt to measure illness rates from a somewhat different perspective. Unfortunately, none of these rates is absolutely specific for illness episodes. For example, it can be seen that married people have substantially more physician visits per year than do never-married individuals. This finding can be interpreted in at least two different ways: 1) that never-married individuals are healthier than married ones, or 2) that married individuals are more concerned with their health status and therefore seek preventive medical care by routine physician visits. Undoubtedly, obstetrical care counts for not only higher rates of physician visits per year but also higher rates of short-term hospitalizations for married people compared with never-married ones.

Leaving these categories aside, Table 5 demonstrates that married and never-married individuals reported fewer days of restricted activity than formerly married people. In general, it can be seen that married people are much healthier than widowed, separated, or divorced ones on all of the health care indicators por-

Table 5. Selected Health Measures, Noninstitutional Civilians, by Marital Status, United States[a]

Date, status	Restricted activity days per person per year	Percent limited in activity because of long-term conditions	Incidence of short-term conditions per 100 persons per year	Physician visits per person per year	Percent with 1 short-stay hospital episode or more during past year
1971–1972					
All persons	18.8	17.0	174.4	5.4	13.0
Married	17.6	15.7	174.4	5.6	14.8
Formerly married					
Widowed	28.1	21.7	165.3	6.2	...
Separated	30.5	24.6	223.5	6.8	18.5
Divorced	26.2	21.7	216.4	6.6	14.6
Never married	17.0	20.6	161.2	4.6	9.1
1976					
All persons	21.2	18.6	182.9	5.3	12.7
Married	20.2	17.5	175.6	5.4	13.5
Formerly married					
Widowed	28.2	24.9	170.7	6.4	16.5
Separated	38.8	27.0	227.6	7.0	17.3
Divorced	30.7	24.4	221.4	6.5	14.5
Never married	19.3	19.8	184.3	4.7	9.3

[a] Aged 17 years and older. Age-adjusted rates include maternity care.
Data from National Center for Health Statistics (10) and unpublished data from the Health Interview Survey.

trayed in Table 5, except for the incidence of short-term conditions in which the widowed fare somewhat better than the married. The comparison of never-married with married individuals is interesting. While the never-married appear to have fewer physician visits per year and lower short-term hospitalization rates, they have more short-term and long-term illnesses than do the married and seem to restrict their activity a bit less than married people do. This pattern, in combination with the fact that fewer never-married individuals have hospital insurance, suggests that although the never-married get sick more often than married individuals, they do not take as good care of themselves, since they do not see physicians as often. Finally, the marital group at greatest risk in all five categories is the separated, who report the highest rates of illness and physician visits (9).

The Somers 1972 and 1976 data were consistent with those presented earlier by Carter and Glick, who conducted a health interview survey during the years 1963–1964 (1). They found that married people were the group most likely to have at least one physician contact during their study year; single people had the lowest rates of physician visits (55.4 percent), while widowed, divorced, and separated people had intermediate rates. In contrast to the physician utilization data, Table 6, taken from the Health

Table 6. Percent with Hospital- and Surgical-Insurance Coverage, for the Civilian Noninstitutional Population Aged 17–64, by Marital Status, Standardized for Age in the United States, July 1962 to June 1963

Marital Status	Persons aged 17 to 64 (in thousands)	Percent with hospital insurance		Percent with surgical insurance	
		Percent	Index	Percent	Index
Married	75,826	77.8	100	72.9	100
Single	16,746	63.7	82	57.3	79
Divorced	2,892	58.9	76	55.2	76
Widowed	3,784	55.8	72	50.9	70
Separated	2,022	45.5	58	40.5	56

From the National Center for Health Statistics: Health Insurance Coverage: United States, July 1962–June 1963. Vital and Health Statistics, Series 10, no. 11. Washington, D.C., U.S. Government Printing Office, 1964 (10).

Interview Survey, indicates that married people are the ones most likely to have health insurance coverage (77.8 percent), followed by single people (63.7 percent). Only 45.5 percent of separated people were covered by hospitalization insurance. The same general pattern holds for dental visits as well, with married and single individuals having the highest utilization rates, and the formerly married having the lowest ones.

Utilizing the 1970 census data as well as the Health Interview Survey, Verbrugge confirmed that divorced and separated individuals continue to have the worst health status associated with the highest rates of acute and chronic conditions as well as disability from health problems (11). The widowed ranked next, followed by singles. In an earlier work, the authors provided summary health care profiles for individuals of various marital status (12).

Divorced and separated people have the worst health status of all marital groups, since they have the highest rates of acute and chronic conditions, suffer the most partial work disability, take the most disability days per condition, especially for injuries, and have the highest average physician utilization rates and the longest hospital stays. They rank second in prevalence of chronic conditions (behind only widowed people) and in complete work disability. Unfortunately, divorced and separated people are the group most likely to have no health insurance coverage.

Widowed people rank second worst for overall health status. They have the highest prevalence rates of chronic conditions and are usually more limited by them. They have the highest percentage of complete work disability, and physician utilization and hospitalization rates are almost as high as for divorced and separated people. The average lengths of hospital stay and of short-term disability per condition are intermediate.

Institutionalization rates for single people are very high, and institutionalization usually occurs at relatively young ages. This group reports the most physical impairments and paralysis. Noninstitutionalized single people appear to be a very healthy group. They have low rates of limiting chronic conditions and conditions that produce work disability. They take the least time off for health problems and have the lowest physician and hospital utilization rates. With the exception of very high injury rates for men, single people usually are unremarkable for the prevalence of acute conditions.

Married people have the best overall health status. They have the fewest acute conditions, chronic limiting conditions, and conditions that produce work disability. They have intermediate rates of chronic conditions, but these illnesses seldom restrict their social involvement. As mentioned before, when compared with the rest of the population, married people have slightly more physician visits per year than the average, which is probably related to obstetrical care.

Remarriage

A number of studies indicate that remarriage plays an important role in health status. In a large survey conducted in Alameda County, California, Renne concluded:

> A large majority of people in our sample who are ever divorced had remarried, and while the remarried as a group tended to be less healthy than people in stable marriages, those who were satisfied with their current marriages reported better health than those who were still involved in unhappy first marriages. In other words, people who had divorced and remarried successfully were less susceptible to health problems than people who had remained in an unhappy marriage. If divorce itself were a symptom of illness signifying physical incapacity, or an inability to sustain close relationships with another person for example, then people who had remarried after divorce would not only have been less satisfied with their marriage, as they were in our sample, but also less healthy in other respects, as they were not, to any significant degree (13, p. 347).

In a large national sample, Weingarten found that on selected indicators of well-being, including a number of psychological and psychophysiological symptoms, remarried individuals compared favorably with those in their first marriages (14). Weingarten mentioned that one difference between first and remarried people was in health care utilization: the remarried were more likely to utilize mental health and other professional services and also tended to report higher levels of chronic stress than did those in first marriages.

Jesse Bernard points out that there are gender differences in the process of remarriage as well as in marriage (15).

Remarriage seems to be a kind of safe conduct voucher for men carrying them through many life stresses. There seems little doubt that having a wife—usually younger and healthier—to take care of the disabilities of aging is a positive factor, not only in male survival, but also in mental health. Equally good health-maintaining care may be available for the never-married and non-remarried only among the fairly affluent. . . . Remarriage does not seem to do as much for women as it does for men; does not seem to have as great survival or mental health significance for them. (p. 562)

Dual Careers and Working Women

Recently, the interaction between health status, marriage, and work for women has been investigated. Northcott, utilizing data from Edmonton, Alberta (more than 750 men and women), found that working married women reported fewer physical and psychosomatic symptoms than either single working women or married women who worked at home (16). Northcott chose to explain this observation with a modified selection hypothesis, that is, that only the healthiest choose to work. The findings suggest that while work may have its liabilities, for married women the benefits outweigh them.

An alternative explanation, ex post facto, is that women who tend to be successful in coping often place themselves into combined marriage, motherhood, and work roles, while women who cope less successfully choose less complicated role situations. According to this reasoning, the relatively low levels of distress reported by working women can be interpreted as reflecting their high coping capabilities, and the relatively high distress reported by women in supposedly less demanding situations can be interpreted as reflecting their more restricted coping capabilities.

A 1976 study concluded that husbands of working women were in poorer health and were less satisfied with their marriages than husbands of full-time housewives, but working women appeared healthier and happier than housewives (17). It was suggested that though employment was beneficial for a working wife, it created strain and illness for the husband because of reduced attention from his spouse and greater demands for sharing duties. A replication study concluded that the wife's employment per se did not cause the illness and strain experienced by her husband; rather, they were due to changes in the wife's employment status such as entering the labor force, receiving a promotion, or leaving employment (18). Carpenter's analysis of the management of family health care by working couples indicated that the burden of family and child health care continued to be borne by women (19). In 1975, the Bureau of Labor Statistics reported that only 10 percent of employed men and 23 percent of employed women reported work absences for illness of other family members. More specifically, only 2 percent of men reported absence from work to care for a child compared with 15 percent of women in the labor force.

Social Explanations of Health Differences by Marital Status

Numerous theories have been proposed to explain the relationship between marital status and health, but the two best known are the selection and protection hypotheses. The selection hypothesis postulates that people who marry and remain married are healthier in the first place than those who either never marry or become widowed, divorced, or separated. Carter and Glick (1) distill the selection hypothesis as follows:

> The process of selection and marriage tends no doubt to leave persons with ill health, in other words, poor mortality risk, among the unmarried. Moreover, they may also leave among the unmarried those who are prone to take more chances that endanger their lives than married persons would ordinarily take in their jobs and in their recreation, because they have no spouse, and probably no children to protect, or because they are so inclined by temperament or longstanding habit. On the other hand, unmarried persons may be overly careful about their health or conduct to the point of withdrawal from the usual forms of sociable contact where potential marital partners would ordinarily be. (p. 344)

The protection hypothesis asserts that marriage creates a safer, more nurturing environment for people, which contributes to their health and speeds their recovery from illness. The structure, routine, and stability of married life, as well as regular diet, intimate human contact, and "something to live for" are all thought to enhance well-being and to combat illness. When illness does occur, marriage permits a person to assume the sick role and recover more completely. Aaron Antonovsky describes marital status as being one of the most important variables in creating a sense of coherence and predictability in the world (20). This sense of coherence ameliorates the impact of stress on the individual.

Both the protection and selection hypotheses have evidence to support them. For example, Verbrugge's, as well as Kobrin and Hendershot's, studies support both hypotheses.

James Lynch very clearly supports the protective aspects of the marriage (21). Lynch indicated that living alone contributed substantially to the secondary gain sought by single people for their illness episodes:

> For many isolated and lonely individuals, illness itself becomes the only legitimate method for getting attention. Many lonely people experience very real secondary gain by getting ill. At least for brief periods of time during hospitalization, they are flooded with compassion provided by hospital staffs, nurses and physicians who care for them, inadvertently providing something that is missing in their lives—human attention. (p. 209)

It would appear that protection and selection operate somewhat independently, and both seem to explain some of the relationship between marital status and health.

Gender Differences

As Bernard pointed out, remarriage (and marriage in general) has a relatively greater benefit for men than for women. By almost any criterion of health, unmarried men fare worse than married men. This observation is true whether one considers data regarding mortality, morbidity, or medical care utilization. Comparisons between married and unmarried women are less consistent.

While married women experience more favorable death rates, the difference is small. Most studies indicate that unmarried women have higher morbidity rates, but they also experience lower hospitalization rates.

The fixed-role and nurturant-role hypotheses have been proposed to explain gender differences in health status, and both are somewhat related to marital status as well. The fixed-role hypothesis was first described by Gove and Tudor (as quoted by Gove [22]).

> The male as household head and particularly as job holder must consistently and satisfactorily meet demands which regularly require him to be involved with his environment. Poor performance by the male is highly visible and will rapidly lead to a lost of roles. In contrast, the role of housewife is relatively unstructured and invisible. It is possible for the housewife to put things off, to let things slide, her husband and/or children may assist her or even take over the running of the home: alternatively the home may simply become extremely messy. The performance of the housewife role depends largely on self-motivation. If the housewife performs poorly, it is unlikely (at least in the short run) that she will lose her role (that her husband will divorce her). For males the presence of structured demands should decrease the likelihood that they would become obsessed with their worries. They are constantly confronting situational demands that must be met and these are apt to draw their attention from personal troubles. In contrast, women are more able to brood over their troubles for their performance is less visible and the demands they confront less structured. This lack of structure allows distress to feed upon itself. (p. 78)

The fixed-role hypothesis has been utilized to explain observed differences between men and women on utilization of medical care. (Women, having freer schedules, also have greater flexibility for access to physicians.)

The nurturant-role hypothesis is not necessarily in conflict with the fixed-role hypothesis. According to Gove (22),

> Women in our society are generally expected to occupy a nurturant role, both performing daily the essential household tasks and taking on the major responsibility for the care of children, spouses and aged relatives. As a consequence, in most living arrangements (1) women

will find it more difficult than men to adopt the sick role completely, and (2) they will tend to experience the demands of others as excessive and as impairing their ability to rest and relax. Thus, as a consequence of their role obligations to others and the corresponding demands others make, women are apt both to become physically run down and to be unable to adopt the sick role successfully. (p. 80)

Both of these hypotheses are currently receiving research attention. However, it seems that both are based upon assumptions which may no longer apply, since greater proportions of women are employed and marital roles are more flexible. Increases in women's employment impacts directly upon the number of women affected by the fixed-role phenomenon and indirectly upon the nurturant-role hypothesis. (With women working out of the home, is the nurturant role diminished or is greater strain placed upon women to do too many things?) The trend toward more working women creates one of the ironies of contemporary life, which has been best described by Lewis and Lewis (23). In an early analysis of the gender health differences, they concluded

If we are striving for a nonsexist society, with equal opportunity for all, it would be better to seek increased opportunities for women in occupation, business and commercial affairs, and a reduction in the morbidity and mortality of men. Perhaps this proposal evades the fundamental question: What is the better measure of equality—for women to die like men, or for men to live (a little bit) like women? Can we not have the benefits of sexual parity in terms of equal opportunities for personal achievement, as well as individual survival? (p. 868)

The progress toward gender equality achieved on social, economic, and occupational fronts may be at the cost of increased health risks. In other words, the sex differential in mortality, which usually favors women and which has been increasing since 1900, may level off or actually decline. There are indications that this is already occurring. Men's life-styles have usually been cited as the major factor adversely affecting their rates relative to women: Men tend to smoke more, they drive cars more, they are more likely to be employed and exposed to occupational risks and the general stresses of working, they tend to have more accidents, and they seem to lead riskier lives. As the working habits of men and women tend to converge, it is likely that the differences in life-styles will become smaller and that women will develop work and life habits which are riskier and less healthy for them. Rates of death due to disease are now declining faster for men than they are for women. Furthermore, in 1963, men were four times as likely to be involved in automobile accidents; but by 1977 the number of women driver had doubled, and women were half as likely as men to have automobile accidents (23). Similarly, the smoking patterns of contemporary women are quite different from those of older cohorts in that smoking has been much more acceptable and common among women who entered adulthood during the 1950s, 1960s, and 1970s. It is estimated that if the trends of the late 1980s continue there will be an equal number of men and women smoking (24).

Thus, all of these four hypotheses—the selection and protection hypotheses and the fixed- versus nurturant-role hypotheses—strongly suggest that life-style is an important factor in determining health status, and marital status is a major component of life-style. Thus, marital therapy may represent one useful approach in helping people manage stress.

EXPLANATORY MECHANISMS

We have reviewed data that demonstrate increased morbidity and mortality following the major life change of divorce or widowhood. It appears that it is the *change* of marital status that produces pathological stress, rather than marital status itself. Examination of Tables 1 and 2 indicates a heterogeneous list of causes of death following divorce or widowhood. It is the purpose of this section to suggest possible mechanisms to help account for the various causes of death.

Figure 3 outlines our hypothetical model of the mechanisms by which marital disruption seems to affect mortality. It appears that there are three major consequences of marital disruption. First, marital disruption has the potential for producing strong negative

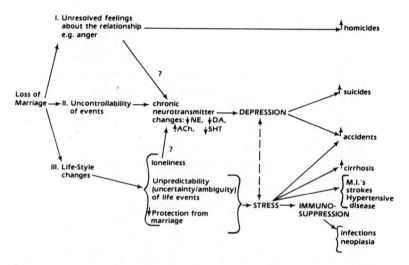

Figure 3. Hypothetical model of mechanisms by which marital disruption affects mortality.

feelings about the relationship, in particular anger, jealousy, guilt, and fear. Some people, especially those with poor ego strength, may have difficulty in coping with these feelings and may act them out against their marital partner. It is possible that these unresolved feelings are related to the increased rates of death due to homicide that are known to occur among divorced persons.

The second possible mechanism is that of depression. While there is little doubt that many divorced and widowed persons experience periods of postmarital depression, the mechanisms that produce the depression are not known with absolute certainty. It would seem that there are at least three possible explanations. 1) Some theorists would suggest that retroflected anger may be related to the onset of depression. 2) Disruption of attachment bonds leading to loneliness may also be an important contributor to depression (25). 3) There appears to be some experimental evidence to suggest that chronic uncontrollability of unpleasant life events is related to changes in levels of neurotransmitters, including depletion of norepinephrine, dopamine, and 5-hydroxytryptamine as well as increases in levels of acetylcholine. All these changes in biogenic amines have been related to depressive symptoms. As Anisman (26) has stated,

> It is our belief that aversive insults may provoke depressive episodes. However, in assessing the relationship between stress and depression it would seem appropriate to consider neurochemical processes as a mediating factor, and cognitive changes, namely, helplessness and hopelessness, as consequences of the neurochemical change. (p. 425)

Of particular interest is the relationship between a person's ability to cope with stress and the onset of neurochemical changes. Again to quote Anisman,

> As indicated earlier, a number of organismic and situational variables will determine the effectiveness of stress in eliciting changes in [norepinephrine] and [5-hydroxytryptamine]. One essential variable in this respect concerns the organism's ability to cope with stress through behavioral means. When behavioral control is possible, [norepinephrine] depletion does not ensue, presumably because the demands placed on endogenous processes are relatively limited. Under conditions where behavioral control is not possible, amine utilization exceeds synthesis resulting in the depletion of the transmitter. Consistent with animal studies, data derived from human experiments have consistently pointed to the possibility that coping failures are fundamental in provoking depression. Indeed, some data have suggested that even if control is not possible, simply the belief that subjects could not experience control over aversive events was sufficient to offset behavioral disruption. (p. 425)

These considerations suggest a differential mechanism to account for variations in morbidity and mortality. It would be expected that individuals who have more control over aspects of their marital disruption would experience less depression and fewer related illnesses than those who have little control. The depression produced by the uncontrollability of events related to marital disruption may be related to the known increase in suicide and accident rates in this population.

Finally, marital disruption is accompanied by major changes in life-style which include 1) loneliness, 2) unpredictability (uncertainty and ambiguity) of life events, and 3) a diminution of whatever protection marriage confers on an individual. We have already mentioned the possible relationship between loneliness and depression. McKinney et al. have suggested that the separation syndrome in monkeys is a valid model for human depression (27), an idea that is consistent with Bowlby's concept of disruption of attachment bonds. Of particular interest is the possibility that loneliness per se may affect immune responsiveness (28). The effects of loneliness are ameliorated mainly by the family of origin, and in general they seem to be particularly severe during the first year after separation. Most people begin to date again within the first postmarital year, and 90 percent do by the second (29).

Marital disruption is known to be stressful. Holmes and Rahe have demonstrated that marital disruption is one of the most stressful life events (30) and that this stress may be related to the *change* of circumstances (31). It is our view that stress is intimately related to fear and anxiety and is often manifested as worry, which represents the anticipation of unpredictable noxious events. Seligman and others have cited evidence to demonstrate the relationship between unpredictability and the presence of anxiety-fear syndromes in animals (32). According to Anisman (26),

> In addition to stress controllability, it seems that stress predictability and feedback for behavioral responses are essential elements in the provocation of some forms of pathology, such as ulceration and myocardial aberrations. These same variables are also believed to influence the perceived aversiveness of events and may contribute to the provocation of depression. (p. 425)

One of the major explanations of the low morbidity and mortality of married individuals is that marriage somehow *protects* people from stress (12). It is felt that routine habits, good nutrition, intimate contact, social support, and something worth living for are all important in conferring this protection. Marital disruption implies that this protection will be removed, thus exposing divorced persons to the full impact of whatever stressors are present. Thus, not only is marital disruption itself unpleasant and therefore stressful, but this stress is accentuated by the lack of marital protection.

The life-style changes secondary to marital disruption lead to stress, which has several consequences. It seems that stress and depression have a close and—some would feel—inseparable relationship. It is beyond the scope of this chapter to enter that discussion. But whether or not one is a proponent of that view, it is clear that marital disruption leads to both states, either independently or not. It is known that rates of death due to accidents of all kinds, including motor vehicle accidents and accidental falls and explosions, are increased among divorced persons and even more so among widowed people. Whether these accidents are due to inattention secondary to stress or represent an alternative form of suicidal behavior secondary to depression is unclear.

Some divorced persons handle the dysphoria related to stress by substance abuse, in particular alcoholism, which would account for the increased rate of death due to cirrhosis of the liver seen in this population. Finally, high levels of stress may increase cardiovascular load, leading to increases in rates of death due to myocardial infarctions, strokes, and hypertensive heart disease.

There is a growing body of literature which indicates that psychosocial factors are related to immunological functioning. The evidence for this has been thoroughly assembled by Jemmott and Locke who conclude, "Consistent with research on lower animals, the bulk of evidence suggests that stress is associated with an increased incidence of diseases against which the immune system defends and that it is associated with diminished immunocompetence as determined in a variety of in vitro assays" (28). They mention considerable evidence that stress is associated with increased incidence of infectious diseases, and they cite numerous studies that relate stress to specific alterations in immune functioning, for example, lower T-lymphocyte responsivity to stimulation in bereaved populations and decreased secretion rates of IgA during periods of stress. Two major neuroendocrine pathways have been proposed to account for the relationship of stress to immune functioning. First, Selye's general adaptation syndrome, and second, Cannon's fight or flight response. To quote Jemmott and Locke,

> In the GAS [general adaptation syndrome], the perception of stress by the cortex and limbic system causes the hypothalamus to release

corticotrophin-releasing factor, which in turn causes the pituitary to release adrenocorticotrophic hormone (ACTH) which stimulates the adrenal cortex to release corticosteroids (e.g., cortisol and corticosterone). In the fight or flight response, the perception of stress produces excitatory activity in the brain stem, resulting in increased sympathetic outflow via the autonomic nervous system. Accompanying this diffuse sympathetic arousal is norepinephrine release at adrenergic nerve endings in target organs and epinephrine release by the adrenal medulla. (p. 96)

There is good research evidence to suggest that while the relationship of corticosteroids and immunity is complicated, in general they are antiinflammatory and immunosuppressive. Increases in cortisol have been associated with decreased lymphocyte responsivity. According to Jemmott and Locke, there is recent evidence that lymphocytes appear to possess receptors for a variety of hormones and neurotransmitters including catecholamines and other stress-related hormones which may have some immunoregulatory function. Stimulation of β-adrenergic (epinephrine) receptors on T lymphocytes, B lymphocytes, and macrophages decreases the cellular response. By contrast, both α-adrenergic (norepinephrine) and cholinergic (acetylcholine) stimulation augment both T- and B-cell responses. There is recent evidence from in vivo human studies that confirms that β-adrenergic drugs are immunosuppressive.

It is of interest that T lymphocytes have recently been shown to have receptors for morphine and met-enkephalin. Morphine appears to have an immunosuppressor effect, and met-enkephalin has an immunoenhancing effect. Furthermore, receptors for β-endorphin have also been identified on lymphocytes and it appears that β-endorphin has an enhancing effect on lymphocyte responsivity.

Thus, it appears that several mechanisms have been elucidated to explain how psychological stress is translated into alterations of immune functioning. These relationships may account for the known increases in rates of death due to infections and neoplasia among bereaved and divorced populations.

We have attempted to describe and explain some of the relationships between marital disruption and health status. It is incumbent on the physician to be particularly alert for health changes among divorced and widowed people. Since widowed people are frequently also elderly, they may be at very high risk for illness in the bereavement period. Aside from closer attention to health status, it may also be judicious to recommend 1) measures aimed at decreasing the unpredictability and uncontrollability of the environment, as well as 2) formation of closer interpersonal relationships, at least temporarily. Since it has been demonstrated that mortality decreases to marital levels when divorced and widowed people remarry, it appears prudent to be cautiously encouraging of peaceful and enjoyable intimate relationships among this group. In Chapter 2, Segraves has reviewed extensive evidence which demonstrates that there is an overrepresentation of the divorced and widowed among psychiatric populations, both inpatient and outpatient. This implies that psychiatrists may increasingly need to assume the role of primary care physician, since this population is at considerable risk for illness. Finally, it may be necessary for psychiatrists to attend carefully to the stress and depression that accompany changes in marital status as independent problems among the patients they are treating for other more traditional psychiatric conditions.

References

1. Carter H, Glick P: Marriage and Divorce: A Social and Economic Study. Cambridge, Harvard University Press, 1970

2. National Center for Health Statistics: Mortality from Selected Causes by Marital Status, Parts A and B. Series 20, no. 8a, 8b, Washington, DC, US Government Printing Office, 1970

3. Kobrin FE, Hendershot GE: Do family ties reduce mortality: evidence from the U.S., 1966–1968. Journal of Marriage and the Family 39:737–745, 1977

4. Veevers JE: Parenthood and Suicide. Social Sci Med [E] 7:135–144, 1973

5. Cox PR, Ford JR: The mortality of widows shortly after widowhood. Lancet 1:163–164, 1964

6. Young M, Benjamin B, Wallace C: The mortality of widowers. Lancet 2:454–456, 1963

7. Parkes CM, Benjamin B, Fitzgerald RG: Broken heart: a statistical study of increased mortality among widowers. Br Med J 1:740–743, 1969

8. Helsing KJ, Szklo M, Comstock GW: Factors associated with mortality after widowhood. Am J Public Health 71:802–809, 1981

9. Somers A: Marital status, health and use of health services. JAMA 241:1818–1822, 1979

10. National Center for Health Statistics: Vital and Health Statistics. Series 10, no. 11. Washington, DC, US Government Printing Office, 1964

11. Verbrugge LM: Marital status and health. Journal of Marriage and the Family 41:267–286, 1979

12. Stewart T, Bjorksten O: Marriage and Health, in Marriage and Divorce: A Contemporary Perspective. Edited by Nadelson CC, Polonsky DC. New York, Guilford Press, 1984

13. Renne K: Health and Marital Experience in an Urban Population. Journal of Marriage and the Family 33:338–348, 1971

14. Weingarten H: Remarriage and well-being. Journal of Family Issues 1:533–560, 1980

15. Bernard J: Afterword. Journal of Family Issues 1:561–571, 1980

16. Northcott HC: Women, work and health. Pacific Sociological Review 23:393–404, 1980

17. Burke R, Weis T: Relationship of wife's employment on marital adjustment and companionship. Journal of Marriage and the Family 38:279–287, 1976

18. Booth A: Wife's employment and husband's stress: a replication and refutation. Journal of Marriage and the Family 39:301–313, 1977

19. Carpenter E: Children's health care and the changing role of women. Med Care 18:1208–1218, 1980

20. Antonovsky A: Health, Stress and Coping. San Francisco, Jossey-Bass, 1979

21. Lynch J: Broken Heart: The Medical Consequences of Loneliness. New York, Basic Books, 1977

22. Gove W: Gender differences in mental and physical illness. Social Sci Med [E] 19:77–84, 1984

23. Lewis C, Lewis M: The potential impact of sexual equality on health. N Engl J Med 297:863–869, 1977

24. National Center for Health Statistics: Vital and Health Statistics, Sex Differences in Health and Use of Medical Care. Series 3, no. 24. Washington, DC, US Government Printing Office, 1983

25. Bowlby J: Grief and mourning in infancy and early childhood, Psychoanal Study Child 15:9–52, 1960

26. Anisman H: Vulnerability to depression: contribution of stress, in Neurobiology of Mood Disorders. Edited by Post RM, Ballenger JC. Baltimore, Williams & Wilkins Co, 1984

27. McKinny WT, Moran EC, Kraemer GW: Separation in nonhuman primates as a model for human depression: neurobiological implications, in Neurobiology of Mood Disorders. Edited by Post RM, Ballenger JC. Baltimore, Williams & Wilkins Co, 1984, pp 393–406

28. Jemmott JB III, Locke SE: Psychosocial factors, immunologic mediation and human susceptibility to infectious diseases: how much do we know? Psychol Bull 95:78–108, 1984

29. Saunders B: The social consequences of divorce: implications for family policy. Journal of Divorce 6:1–17, 1983

30. Dohrenwend BS, Dohrenwend BP (eds): Stressful Life Events and Their Nature and Effects. New York, John Wiley & Sons, 1974

31. Fenwick R, Barresi CM: Health consequences of marital-status change among the elderly: a comparison of cross-sectional and longitudinal analyses. J Health Soc Behav 22:106–116, 1981

32. Seligman M: Learned Helplessness. San Francisco, WH Freeman and Co, 1975

4

Second Marriages

Clifford J. Sager, M.D.

4

Second Marriages

Remarried couples are those in which one or both partners were previously married to someone else, and were either divorced or widowed. The partners may or may not have children from the previous marriage. These couples as a group are distinct from couples married for the first time. Seventy-five percent of divorced women and 83 percent of divorced men do remarry. There are strong motivations and pressures to do so, despite having had one or more marriages end. Treatment of marital dysfunction is based on a variety of theoretical concepts that in turn spawn an even greater number of therapeutic techniques and approaches. The techniques and theory of treating remarried couples does not differ appreciably from dealing with troubled first marriage couples, but several additional factors make the situation more complex. Our focus will be on these additional variables and considerations. The most important of these factors are as follows:

1. Either one or both partners had married previously. The ending

The author is grateful to his colleagues at the Jewish Board of Family and Children's Services in New York City, Holly Steer Brown, Helen Crohn, Tamara Engel, Evelyn Rodstein, and Libby Walker, who with him, are authors of the more complete report [Treating the Remarried Family, Brunner/Mazel] on our work with remarried families.

of that marriage leaves scars, caveats, and bonds that affect the relationship of the second couple.

2. More likely than not, the couple start their married life with an instant family: the children of either one or of both. There has been little time to consolidate the marriage, as the presence of children and the necessity of their care are immediate.

3. There may be no children from previous marriages. Research of Pasley and Ihinger-Tallman (1) on a nonclinic population confirms that serious marital relationship problems for this group are much fewer than for those with children. Remarriage with stepchildren is a more complex and hazardous undertaking.

4. When emotional divorce (as differentiated from legal divorce) is incomplete, the former spouse can present problems for the remarried couple that do not exist for the first-married. Former lovers do not seem to have the same carry-over impact as a former spouse of several years with whom one has produced children.

5. Children have only one biological parent in the remarried family. They have not had a lifelong history with the stepparent, whose entry onto the child's scene disturbs the postdivorce adaptation between child and biological parent. Divided loyalties between the biological parent of the same gender as the stepparent provide additional possibilities for friction.

6. The spouses' life-cycle positions, and hence needs and desires, are more likely to be disparate in second marriages than in first marriages.

7. In a first marriage, the couple's income is spent for the family unit and planned for the family unit. In remarriage, financial decisions have been made by courts. Agreements were made with a previous spouse that had been influenced by guilt, ambivalence, or pressure. These later limit the money at the disposal of the remarried couple for their unit. As a corollary, the child support to a mother may be insufficient, causing a problem between her and her new spouse.

Pasley and Ihinger-Tallman (1) group problems in remarried

families (and remarriages) in three domains: 1) behavior and expectations related to merging different family "cultures" or value systems; 2) behaviors and expectations related to merging different perceptions regarding rules of resource distribution (for example, time, energy, and affection); and 3) behaviors and expectations related to merging previously established and currently expected loyalty bonds. These authors suggest that problems found in these domains act as constraints to optimum functioning and satisfaction in remarried families. It is our belief that these constraints directly affect the marital pair and the quality of the marriage.

THEORETICAL MODEL

Our theoretical model for evaluation and therapy provides a matrix for understanding the couple and the sources of their conflicts, and it also clarifies points for therapeutic entry. It is based on the marriage contract concept (2–4), the interactional contract or script of the couple (2), and the behavioral profiles (2, 3). We are concerned with the couple as a system (as well as with the other systems that impinge on the marital system), with the life cycles of each partner and how these affect the remarried marital and family life cycles, and with the individual psychodynamic strengths and frailties of each spouse. These factors can be summarized as systems–cycles–psyche (4).

These theoretical constructs provide an overall systemic understanding of the dynamics of intimate relationships as well as an automatic descriptive diagnosis of the interactional pattern of the couple. Other factors not included in this scheme contribute to the total picture, but so much is included that the scheme does provide an excellent working basis. The marriage contract reminder list has been adopted for remarried couples (4) and is included as Appendix A at the end of this chapter.

Following is a brief summary of the above three concepts—the marriage contract, the interactional contract, and the behavioral profiles—that form the basis for evaluation and therapy. For further details, we refer the reader to the original comprehensive works on this subject and to its adaptation to remarriage situations (2, 4).

The Marriage Contract

The marriage contract is really a misnomer. It does not refer to formal contracts or agreements that mates have drawn up together, that they fully understand, and that they have signed with an expectation of permanence. Instead, each partner has his or her vague awareness of terms that he believes his or her spouse has agreed to. The two mates' contracts are usually quite different. Each contract consists of conscious and unconscious expectations of the relationship, of what the individual wants from his or her partner and what he or she will give in return. Some of the terms in each contract may be at odds with others, thus producing inconsistency so that contradictory messages are given to the spouse. For example, one partner may insist on being independent, yet require the spouse's approval for all of his or her actions. When one partner perceives or senses that the spouse is not fulfilling the terms of the contract (of course, the partner may not be aware of the terms), the partner then tries to correct the breach of the contract by reacting in characteristic ways, such as becoming angry, being irritable for apparently unknown reasons, withdrawing, developing psychosomatic symptoms, or having the wish to escape.

The reminder list of the marriage contract (Appendix A) presents categories of areas that are common in contracts. The purpose of this list is to remind the partners to consider whether these are significant areas in their relationship. The first category deals with expectations of the remarriage and includes such items as help in dealing, caring for, and disciplining the children; companionship, love, and a relief from the world of the formerly married; and provision of an immediate, ready-made family.

The second category is based on psychological and biological needs that the mate is expected to fulfill. These include: relationship modifications with one's own children; ties to the former spouse; questions regarding closeness-distance needs; power and control; inclusion-exclusion of others; how partners deal with anxiety, nurturing and affection, specific aspects of sexual needs, and cognitive styles.

The third category deals with areas of complaints that couples have. The complaints appear to be the cause of the marital problem; however, they more often are the external manifestations or problems that are rooted in the first two categories. Communication, life-style, money, and child-rearing problems often appear here. It is often wise in treatment to shift a specific complaint into its more generic form; for example, money problems often should be shifted to power struggles, where they can often be dealt with more effectively.

In a broad sense the therapist's task is to move the couple toward a single contract whose terms are known to both partners. There need not and cannot be complete agreement on every term. Differences are to be respected, and compromises and quid pro quos are worked out.

The Interactional Contract

In the interactional contract or script, the two partners collaborate to establish and maintain a method of achieving sufficient gratification of their biological and psychological needs as well as their adult and remaining infantile wishes. To remain viable, the marriage must accomplish this without arousing so much defensive anxiety or aggression that the marriage as a unit capable of fulfilling its goals and purposes is destroyed. The interactional contract deals with how a couple together tries to fulfill each partner's separate goals and purposes. It is the how, not the what.

Individual contracts help the therapist understand the ingredients that contribute to the couple's interactional system. In their interaction, both partners are usually unaware of nonverbal, as well as verbal expressions, that contribute to the quality of their interaction. This interactive contract provides the operational field in which each struggles with the other to achieve fulfillment of his or her own individual contract, including all the realistic, unrealistic, and ambivalent clauses that it contains. It is the place where each partner tries to achieve his or her own objectives and force the other to behave in accordance with his or her own design of the marriage.

The interactional contract is unique for each couple because it evolves from the most basic wishes and striving, as well as the defensive maneuvers, of each partner. Each spouse stimulates defensive maneuvers in the other that may or may not be characteristic of that partner in another relationship.

Much of therapy consists of making the interactional contract and the partners' behavior in it more conscious. The increased consciousness on the part of both spouses automatically works toward their arriving at a new single contract that provides the basis for healthier interactions, interactions that will fulfill reasonable objectives and purposes. Since the goals of the marriage are determined by the couple, the clauses of the individual contracts come into the foreground and have to be dealt with. The therapist tries to make clear the salient positive and negative aspects of each contract so that each partner can resolve conflicting and ambivalent clauses within it. Awareness is not necessarily a prerequisite for change, but willingness to make the effort to change is necessary.

Contractual Difficulties

For remarried couples the primary source of contractual difficulties is usually that one or both contracts are based on unrealistic expectations of the new marriage or spouse. If unrealistic expectations are focused on the marriage, the significant expectations of each partner are mutually exclusive. If the unrealistic expectations are focused on the spouse, one partner may fulfill his or her obligations, but his or her own needs remain unfulfilled because the spouse does not have the capacity to fulfill them, is not aware of the partner's wishes, or may deny perception of them if they have been clearly expressed. Expectations may be based on idealizations that no relationship could fulfill.

Behavioral Profiles

Certain styles of behaving or adapting are often found grouped together for an individual. I have summarized these in a shorthand called behavioral profiles (2). How one's behavioral profile fits or interacts with that of the mate is a useful way to think about some possible marital and remarriage pairings.

The behavioral profile refers to the prevalent way in which one mate relates to the other. There is fluidity and change in immediate situations, but over a period of time, a dominant pattern can be discerned. Profiles for any individual may vary markedly with different mates or at different times in the marital life cycle. In 60 percent of remarriages, the remarried partner's profile with the present spouse will be different from that partner's profile with the first spouse.

Seven behavioral profiles emerge that describe different behavioral approaches of each partner to the other. The behavioral profiles, although similar in some way to Berne's parent, adult, and child designations (5) are modes that do not change as rapidly as Berne's.

Any of the following profiles may be considered normal and socially acceptable behavior. However, when extrapolated beyond a certain point, any of these patterns become pathological.

Equal Partner. The equal partner wants equality for self and partner. He or she tends to be cooperative and independent. An equal partner is capable of sustained intimacy without clinging and is able to share or assume decision making and to allow the mate to do the same. An equal partner gives and accepts love. He or she is relatively free of infantile needs that must immediately be fulfilled. Furthermore, he or she does not believe that his or her lovability depends on skillfulness in fulfilling the infantile needs of a mate. At appropriate times the equal partner can be either parental or childlike but is not "stuck" in either position.

Equal partner combinations can be highly adaptive for remarriage. An equal partner would be able to share a mate, as needed, with children. Personal satisfaction would not come only through the mate. There would be flexibility in roles as required by remarriage, there would be respect for differences in such areas as child rearing, values, and life-styles. Love and commitment would not be founded on a fear of loss or abandonment. An equal partner could take the necessary time to work through a step-relationship with a mate's children, while being able to tolerate not receiving immediate reciprocal affection.

Romantic Partner. The romantic partner is dependent on a mate. He or she feels incomplete without a partner. Sentiment and anniversaries are extremely important. Such a partner is likely to be possessive and controlling, and is vulnerable if the spouse refuses to play a reciprocal romantic role. The spouse must be a soul mate with similar values and reactions. Great value is placed on the intensity of love and the passion of sex as criteria for the relationship's success.

Two romantic partners can be very successful as a couple. However, in remarriage, the children may be left "parentless," they may be left to raise themselves, or they may be subtly excluded from the home because the adults are preoccupied with their togetherness. A romantic partner in combination with an equal partner may create problems in the marriage if the romantic partner pushes for a great deal of togetherness and exclusivity. The romantic partner's mate's involvement with children of a former marriage, with an ex-spouse, with friends, or with a career can be extremely threatening.

Parental Partner. A parental partner relates to the mate as to a child. Behavior may range from very controlling and authoritative to mildly patronizing. It may be benign and rewarding or harsh, punitive, and authoritarian. There is a need to dominate the mate to assure the parental partner that he or she is needed and is therefore "loved." Torvald in Ibsen's *The Doll's House* is the prototype, as the early Nora is the prototypic childlike partner.

Particularly relevant for remarriage is one subtype of the parental partner known as the "rescuer" who frequently teams up with a "save-me." This partnership is a relatively unstable and transient one that often begins to crumble after the rescue is over.

Other types of parental partners can function well in remarriage, particularly if they act as benevolent parents to their mate and children. A highly positive grounding can be provided for the family as long as the parental partner is not challenged by the mate or children in terms of authority and control, or as long as there is no threat of abandonment. In remarriage, parental partners may function well with their mates but function poorly with preadolescent and adolescent children when they try to grasp authority too quickly.

Childlike Partner.   This partner complements the parental partner. The childlike partner seems to encounter the most difficulty when competing with stepchildren for care and attention. These partners find the presence of stepchildren threatening to their position with the new spouse, and are unable to meet the children's needs for parenting. Childlike-childlike partnerships, the "sandbox marriage," can function over a short range but are unstable for the long run. Crises develop and each partner wants the other to be the parent, but neither accepts the parental role.

Rational Partner.   The rational partner tries to establish a reasoned, logical, well ordered relationship with responsibilities of partners well defined. He or she forms a close and emotionally dependent relationship but cannot see that emotions influence behavior. This partner is often more dependent than he or she appears to be. Underneath the rational partner's logic, there are genuine feelings of closeness and affection for the mate, as compared with the parallel partner (discussed below) who may be emotionally out of touch with the spouse.

The rational partner's sense of order can be positive in remarriage, but he or she may also find the complexity and fluidity difficult to take. We often see that such partners are confused and at odds with their stepchildren's responses to their approach. The rational partner often acts as a steadying sail for a more volatile one, while the latter serves as the first partner's emotion expressor, one whom the rational partner can gently censure for going too far or being too enthusiastic when the rational partner's anxiety is aroused.

Companionate Partner.   The companionate partner seeks to ward off loneliness and to establish a relationship that need not include romantic love or passion but does include thoughtfulness, loyalty, and kindness given to, and desired from, the partner. The companionate partner wants married life, but may be afraid to love again. When love is demanded there can be problems. Often companionate partners will carefully work out financial agreements and other arrangements for a second marriage.

Problems arise at times from a tendency to live with too many reminders of an idealized past love-marriage or to make comparisons with a former mate. Although it often starts as a marriage of convenience and accommodation, the companionate marriage can blossom into a very gratifying relationship for both partners. Older couples with adult children often have problems dealing with the allocation of current parental funds, as well as designations in wills. At times the couple's attachment to each other, and their annoyance with children who are more concerned with their inheritance than their parent's happiness and security, push the couple closer together.

Parallel Partner.   The parallel partner interacts with his mate to avoid an intimate relationship. He desires distance and emotional space and maintains all the forms of an intimate home, but emotionally is not close. The partners' lives run parallel, rather than intertwined. His or her need to maintain distance usually stems from a fear of becoming merged with and controlled by a partner.

In remarriages where children are involved and the demands of the complex interrelationships call for more than superficial involvement, the parallel partner may constantly feel invaded by the rest of the family. A woman parallel partner may resent the demands of being stepmother to her mate's children and may fear that these demands would take over her life. She tends to remain distant, but she completes in good form those things that have to be done. The male parallel partner may dump his children on his wife, with the desire to pursue "his own thing." If pressed too hard to be intimate, sensing the severe threat to his homeostasis, the parallel partner will escape marital relationships.

In describing partnerships, the convention is to use the husband's profile first and hyphenate it to the wife's. For example, a romantic-equal marriage would indicate a romantic partner husband with an equal partner wife. The typology does not attempt to note the degree of conflict, the positive or negative complementarity, or the motivation of the couple. In most instances, there is a secondary set of profiles that emerges under certain conditions. It is this second set, along with complementarity, that often makes it possible for a marriage to survive that otherwise would not. Behavioral profiles can and do change. The therapist helps the couple find better adaptations for fulfilling their goals and clears the way for changing some terms in the marriage contract to arrive at a single one that both partners can agree upon. This work is usually conducted only partially on a cognitive level.

The marriage contract concept, along with the interactional contract and behavioral profiles, is helpful in understanding couple dynamics and suggesting points and approaches for therapeutic intervention. It is important to consolidate the couple relationship if the remarried family is to begin coping with its family tasks. In therapy, this consolidation is often the first target for therapeutic work and the quickest way to reduce chaos in the family.

MOTIVATIONS TO REMARRY

Divorce, in contrast to widowhood, is a volitionally created state. It is an act on the part of one or both spouses to terminate a marriage and to seek a better life. This goal may or may not include a new partner, but for most formerly married persons, it does.

Many of the motivations to marry again are similar to those

that motivate people to marry the first time. People, for the most part, elect to live with a mate of the opposite sex, whom they initially love, in order to bear and raise children, seek emotional and financial security, and build a support and living system around themselves. We will focus on those motivations that are more common among the remarried and the never-before-married who select a divorced or widowed mate, who may or may not have children. It is important to examine motivations because they affect conscious and unconscious expectations of one's partner and of the relationship.

In Chapter 2 of this monograph, Dr. Segraves extensively reviews the relationship of marital status to mental health. His findings suggest that many adults who have been married have such a strong need to have a unique mating relationship that they tend to be emotionally disturbed if they are not so connected. There may be a slightly higher rate of basic emotional disturbance among those who divorce or who have been divorced, but there is no firm evidence to support this. (In fact, it is perhaps evidence of mental health to leave a marriage that is rife with disharmony than to have a chronically ill, psychiatrically disabled, or hospitalized spouse.) Divorced persons remarry or live together in a committed relationship with someone else, recognizing their desire for connubial life and reciprocated love. Some seek to provide a parent surrogate for children. If their original marital relationship had been a good one and they were deeply in love, they may masochistically choose a spouse who could not possibly be a suitable partner. The dynamic involved is a variation of incomplete divorce and avoidance of mourning. In these instances, people remain "loyal" to their love by deliberately (unconsciously and sometimes even consciously) marrying someone whom they recognized they can never love. The commonplace rationalization is, "If I work at it, I can love him (or her) enough; I know it will work out OK." It doesn't, and it adds to the list of unsuccessful remarriages.

Motivations to remarry are important because they are often the basis for terms in one partner's marriage contract that the other is unaware of, or, if aware, did not comprehend the operative significance of. An example would be a formerly single woman

who agrees with her older spouse's desire that they not have
children together.

EVALUATING THE MARITAL SYSTEM

Whether the remarried couple requests help with a child-centered
problem (as 56 percent do) or place the difficulty within their own
relationship (27 percent) (Sager CJ, Santaella W, unpublished data),
it is usually essential to evaluate the marital relationship. Family
sessions or separate couple's interviews often reveal marital stress
that had not been mentioned as a presenting complaint. The
therapist has to be sensitive to the spouses' reluctance to perceive
or acknowledge flaws in their relationship, since they are fearful
of another marital failure. Scapegoating a child or a former spouse
supports each spouse's denial and preserves their whistling-in-the-
dark pseudomutuality. One may find that these fears lead couples
to conceal information about previous relationships from the therapist, other family members, or both. Developing a genogram (or
genealogical diagram) with the couple will often bring secret prior
relationships into the open and disclose intergenerational problems and events.

When a remarried couple presents with marital difficulty, the
clinician can often begin to work with the couple alone, although
it is wise to have at least one family session to assess the total
family picture. It is usually contraindicated to involve former
spouses in the assessment or early phase of the treatment program
if complaints focus on the present couple's interaction. Later, a
former spouse may need to be involved if the emotional divorce is
not complete, or if parent-child relationships are problematic.

The concepts of individual marital contracts and typologies
provide a perspective from which to understand couples' problems. While use of the reminder list of contractual terms itself
may not be appropriate in the evaluation stage of every couple, the
parameters it describes can help the clinician develop hypotheses
about the couple's interaction, complementarity, and conflicts.

A reminder list designed for use by couples is included in
Appendix A. It can be given to some couples to talk through

together. They then write down the significant items and detail their differences. For other couples, particularly those who cannot discuss things together without ending in a pitched battle, it is wiser to ask them to write out their responses separately and discuss them in the conjoint sessions when the therapist can better control their interactions.

In understanding the remarried couple, the following parameters are particularly pertinent:

1. Expectations regarding the spouses' relationship to one another's children;
2. Expectations about decision-making processes, duties, responsibilities, and tasks of the family and/or how these will be guided by the couple;
3. Expectations regarding the handling of money and responsibilities for financial support;
4. Expectations regarding the inclusion or exclusion of members of the remarried family suprasystem and the inclusion or exclusion of noncustodial children;
5. Expectations regarding closeness-distance and autonomy-dependence;
6. Differences in the place of each spouse in his or her individual life cycle and each spouse's willingness and ability to fulfill an appropriate role in the marital and family life cycles (4, 6);
7. Anxieties about another marital failure, how these fears are handled or denied, and how each partner reacts to the fears of the others;
8. Fears of loneliness or abandonment; and
9. How the former relationship impinges on the present one; transference-like reactions developed in relation to the former spouse and shifted to the present one.

In the process of evaluating the remarried couple, the therapist elicits significant marital contract material either during sessions or by having the couple talk through the items on the reminder list. In doing this, the clinician organizes the material, which usually promotes understanding and subsequently relief in spouses who often are confused, angry, accusatory, and unable to "get a handle" on what went amiss. In the initial stages of evaluation, we use joint interviews, as well as at least one split session for individual interviews with each spouse. The individual interviews are important to elicit each partner's motivation to continue the marriage, covert activities, conduct in the past that each may wish to hide, degree of emotional desire for previous partners, and extramarital relations.

A three-generation (at least) genogram should be done with all spouses. It is essential to determine the extent of emotional divorce from former spouses and whether appropriate mourning of the lost relationship, home, affluence, or life-style has been completed. Without acceptance of the loss and readiness for the new marriage, the relationship has two strikes against it.

The "instant family" and "love of stepchildren" are myths of remarriage that prepare the way for the equally disastrous and self-fulfilling myths of the wicked step-parent. Consolidation of the marital relationship is the central force that determines the quality of the remarried family's functioning and well-being. Hence, it is a top priority in treatment.

Goals of therapy are established with the couple. Goals may be immediate, intermediate, and long range. It is important to help the couple arrive at goals that are reasonable and possible to achieve.

THERAPEUTIC PRINCIPLES AND TECHNIQUES

The therapist who has had training and experience in individual, group, marital, and family modalities is at an advantage when working with remarried couples. Knowledge of and experience with a variety of theoretical approaches is most helpful. The approaches we have found to be most useful are a *general systems theory* approach to understand family structure and interaction, psychoanalytic theory to help understand individual dynamics and their reciprocating relationship with family dynamics, and learning theory with its therapeutic application, behavior therapy.

Use of the Marriage Contract

The marriage contract makes understandable what the marital conflict is about on superficial as well as intrapsychic and couple-system levels. When couples present the clinician with typical complaints about money, sex, time, past injuries, child rearing, former spouses, or friends, the use of the contract concept makes it possible for the therapist to go beyond these complaints to more basic issues which may include power, inclusion-exclusion, closeness-distance, and passive-assertive parameters, absence of love or caring, and others. Thus, the therapist is in a better position to determine whether to deal with the symptom or with the common etiological factor that may cause several symptoms to surface. The therapist familiar with a range of theories, techniques, and modalities has greater information with which to develop a treatment plan that is most likely to achieve the desired goals. The concepts are ones that are demystifying for clients, who are relieved to gain understanding of why and how they deal with one another, which contributes to their hope for and desire to change. In those cases in which a decision is reached to terminate the relationship, it is much more salutary for partners to know why they cannot (or do not) want to work on trying to make it together.

Contracts are useful not only for purposes of diagnosis but also to help guide the ongoing treatment program and to cue the therapist to productive areas for intervention. The interactional scripts provide a rich focal area for intervention where communication, strategic, and structural techniques for changing dysfunctional interactions can be utilized most profitably.

Early in treatment we usually start to orient spouses to work toward a single contract as a means to achieve a better relationship. Often this is at first done implicitly, as the couple and therapist compare the terms of the two separate contracts that have been verbalized or written out by the couple. In its broadest sense, the road we travel along toward the goal of a single contract *is* the work of therapy. As stated by Sager in an earlier work (2), the terms of the contract must be the choice of the two spouses, not of the therapist.

The clinician tries to be a guide, a facilitator, a remover of road blocks, drawing the couple's attention to the problem areas as well as those that are congruent and complimentary. The therapist devises tasks to change their behavior towards each other, and interprets their intra-psychic and system dynamics to them when that will help. The present is related to the past; to their parents' marriage and their relationship with their parents, to their role assignments in their family of origin, to their relationship with siblings and how this may affect their current marital behaviors, and to other life experiences when any of this is indicated. The therapist manipulates their system on their behalf, with their consent and cooperation. (p. 196)

The therapist may elect not to verbalize the marriage contract but can use it as a framework for organization of the data. With some couples the concept may be utilized in sessions, with the therapist raising questions from the reminder list that may be seminal sources of couple dysfunction. For others, the therapist may give the reminder list to the couple or develop a (briefer, perhaps) reminder list or check-off paper-and-pencil instrument. It is a flexible concept that can be employed in many ways.

Although all the elements in the new single contract may not please each spouse, the single contract is based on quid pro quos that the spouses agree upon and find acceptable without one feeling defeated or overwhelmed by the other. The agreements the spouses develop have to be ones that are possible to fulfill. Like all dynamic agreements, they require periodic renegotiation.

Differences between spouses are usual. There is no need to have to act, feel, or look alike; but the couple must respect their differences and still accept each other. The way love and affection are expressed is often an area that requires attention. Spouses are prone to fail to see an expression of love when that love is not offered in a style they know well.

In working therapeutically with the remarried couple, the clinician makes use of general marital, family, and individual therapy skills, as well as an awareness of the special issues that distinguish a remarriage from a first marriage. With some couples, an educational, group-guidance, or self-help approach may supply the needed support and open enough vistas to make marital therapy per se unnecessary. In therapy we address ourselves to the plight of those remarried couples whose fundamental differences and difficulties indicate the need for more than an educational approach.

Modalities

Most work with remarried couples is conjoint, but this does not exclude the possibility of seeing the couple with their children, individually, with an ex-spouse, with their suprafamily system members, or in groups with other couples.

Remarried couple groups have proven to be especially effective because the group allows the spouses time to focus on themselves and their relationship. In the group, couples are free from the focus on children. This freedom can be anxiety-producing but rewarding. Since there are several (usually four) couples in the group, there is enough pressure and a common desire to "leave the children out of it," "not blame the children." Couples see in the group that they are not unique, that other people share their problems. The group process can take some of the heat out of issues, as well as lead to productive problem-solving and the modeling of solutions.

Most meaningful to couples in group therapy is their sensitivity to one another's feelings and situations, and their ability to approach difficult topics: sex, money, and their feelings about their living or deceased, former and current, spouses. The remarried couples group experience is part of a total treatment plan for each of these families, which usually includes some marital work prior to the group. As shown in the following example, the group might be used to move the couple out of a deadlock or off a plateau that has developed during couples therapy.

Case Example 1

Mr. and Mrs. S. had lived together for five years. Mrs. S. complained, "Saul is too harsh with his daughters; they're only 11 and 14. He's too arbitrary and ready to be angry with them. I'm glad they only visit one day a weekend. It upsets me to see what he does to them." Mr. S.

thought that his wife exaggerated and added, "How would she know? She doesn't have children and doesn't want any." He then became silent.

Mr. S. was extremely guarded in couples sessions. He denied being aware of any feelings and answered tersely. Mrs. S., too, was guarded, but somewhat less so. Communication between them and with the therapist was sparse and nonrevealing. The therapist was unable to get them past their communication impasse. The couple reluctantly accepted the recommendation to join a remarried couples' open-ended group that met on weeks alternating with their own couples sessions. It was felt that the group would be an excellent alternative treatment modality for a number of reasons: the pressure would not be on them to produce; they might find it easier to speak up for other persons in the group than for themselves; they might see that their problems were shared by others; and the peer process of the group would add an important ingredient beyond that of the authority of the therapist.

Mr. and Mrs. S. set their own cautious pace in getting involved in the group. After six weeks Mr. S. expressed his anger to a woman in the group because he felt she was being insensitive to her husband's feelings. This led to other members safely being able to penetrate the couple's lowered defenses, and information began to emerge that Mrs. S. came from a home in which she had been mentally and physically abused. She identified with a man in the group who had abused his children. (The therapist now hypothesized that some of Mrs. S.'s reaction to her husband's criticism of his daughters was a positive identification with his girls and a reaction formation to her own aggressive impulses.)

Mr. S. heard the experiences of women in the group who had raised their children alone. This opened the way for him to understand better his former wife and his daughters. Over nine months these two closed-off partners became group members who gave to and received from the group, one another, and others in their lives. They became increasingly effective coparents, and their own relationship became gratifying.

This case illustrates, too, the use of the multimodal approach; in this instance, couples sessions and remarried couples' group therapy. There is also the option to include the children with the couples' group for a few sessions when problems and ages of the children are roughly similar. Children, particularly adolescents, sometimes meet in their own group.

There are no hard and fast rules for determining modalities, or when to combine them or to change to another. We prefer to work with the remarried couple because of their central role in the remarriage family, and because of their need to consolidate their relationship and to avoid scapegoating others. However, we freely use some individual sessions to work through an impasse or to involve children in the therapy program as their needs indicate.

SPECIAL PROBLEMS OF REMARRIED COUPLES

The Former Spouse

In addition to the clinician's sensitivity to how remarried spouses are influenced by their families of origin, there needs to be sensitivity to how the current marriage is influenced by the past and present relationship with the former spouse. We ask remarried couples to include in their individual marital contracts information about their previous marriages. We are particularly interested in whether the relationship to the new spouse is different from or similar to that with the former spouse, and whether there has been growth in terms of a more mature mate choice, affect, and behavior. A discussion of the former marriage or relationship is necessarily a charged one for both persons, and therefore the clinicians need to be sensitive to this; at the same time, clinicians must be comfortable themselves with the emotions this material may elicit. All too often clinicians avoid talking about former marriages, and collude with clients in denying that they have importance or even that they ever existed.

The feelings about the former spouse, both expressed and unexpressed, may span the spectrum from very active hostility, anger, and denigration; to passivity, "no feelings," and neutrality; to guilt, self-blame, continued mild affection, love, and a desire or fantasy of reuniting "some day" and of having regular or sporadic sex together. These feelings, attitudes, and behaviors may reflect a lack of mourning for the former spouse and appropriate closure of the former relationship. Talking through and recognizing both the positive and negative aspects of that former life and "laying to rest" the past, insofar as possible, can deflect or neutralize the intrusion of the past relationship.

It is often helpful for the couple to look at 1) how the past relationship is being projected into the present, 2) the way their own behavior duplicates the past and stimulates a similar response from their present mate, and 3) the way one can overreact when there is something (positive or negative) in the present relationship that conjures up the past spouse. One has to ask whether either spouse tries to "force" the mate into behaving as the ex-spouse had. A period of testing often takes place in courtship, but as time goes on, some mates push harder to bring forth negative reactions. Sensing this and unconsciously wanting to comply, partners will often fall into behaving as their partners "demand"—even to their own disadvantage. A subtle struggle often goes on as to which mate will press the other into his or her procrustean bed.

A special variation of "the first spouse who has not been put to rest" is seen sometimes when a person marries "for the children," but marries someone whom he or she cannot love, because the "true" love for the former spouse continues. These marriages do not stand much of a chance to be gratifying for the children or either remarried spouse.

In dealing with the issue of the former spouse, the clinician should be aware of how much the ex-spouse intrudes into the new marriage, both physically, by being close by or by making frequent phone calls, and symbolically, in the form of furniture, dishes, or even the conjugal bed that may have been in service in a previous marriage. Children are often perceived as a representation of the former spouse. A dramatic example of this took place in a multifamily therapy session (made up of five remarried families). The mother of a 16-year-old daughter who strongly identified this child with her former husband who had deserted her stated, "You are like two peas in a pod—you're just like him."

Sometimes friends are tolerated who are loyal to the ex-spouse and do not accept the new marriage. All this contributes to the new spouse's sense of being on the "outside" rather than truly paired with the new mate. The spouse may unwittingly encourage this reaction by staying on the telephone too long with the former spouse unnecessarily, talking too intimately, being avidly solicitous—all ostensibly to stay on the good side of the former spouse so that there would be no interference with child visitation, or for some other reason.

These common remarried couple complaints about inclusion-exclusion do not occur in first marriages in the same way. Intrusion by a mother-in-law or father-in-law is just not the same as intrusion by an ex-spouse, as destructive as the first two may be. Surface complaints usually relate to the remarried spouses' deeper mutual expectations of each other, what each one wants to give and receive in return. For example, one mate's involvement with the ex-spouse may be an expression of his expectation in the current relationship in terms of independence or distance from the current spouse. The current spouse may have expected the new husband or wife to "drop" the former spouse so they could become a close-knit couple devoting much time and energy to each other. The couple can renegotiate their expressed and unexpressed expectations of each other in this area, but in remarriage there is still the reality of having to deal with the existence of and need for contact with the ex-spouse in some way. This becomes doubly necessary as we believe in continued coparenting by both biological parents.

What the new spouse does vis-à-vis the former spouse affects the current pairing. It is important when one or both adults of a new marriage have been married previously that they do not deny their history. One's children and former spouses can't be wished away. The remarried are not innocents. When faced, the historical reality need not negatively affect the new relationship; its denial, however, can be a most serious negative prognostic sign.

When an ex-spouse is damaged in some way, physically or emotionally, or perhaps has not set himself or herself up in a satisfactory life situation, the potential for serious problems exists. Often, the spouse, out of guilt, feels that he or she has to rescue or accommodate the former mate, for fear of damaging that former spouse or the children further. To go overboard in this direction is not unusual.

Case Example 2

Mr. B.'s former wife, who had been in a mental hospital several times since their divorce 10 years earlier, came twice a week to the apartment where he lived with his second wife and son to visit with their son. The reason for her visits was to spare the son having to see the poor living conditions of his mother, who still resided in a furnished room, although she could afford better. Mr. B. did not feel his ex-wife could cope with any other visiting arrangement and was hesitant to confront her for fear she would "fly off the handle." The present Mrs. B. felt these visits were an unnecessary intrusion into their home and resented the former Mrs. B. for helping herself to food and leaving dirty dishes.

In the couples sessions, it became clear that both Mr. and Mrs. B. felt invaded by his former wife. The couple had polarized around the issue, with the present Mrs. B. being the focal, complaining, "bad" one and her husband the "good," calm, soothing, moderating one. In addition to the concrete issue of how to deal with the intrusion, the former spouse's visits had become the focus for a negative marital interactional script for the B.'s

After some discussion, which at one point included Mr. B.'s adolescent son, a less corrosive way of handling the ex-spouse's visits was considered. Mr. B. was able to relate his unwillingness to confront his ex-wife with his own anger at her illness and ineffectiveness as a mother, and also his extreme guilt for having divorced her. His guilt also invaded the relationship with his son, whom he was unable to confront when the boy truanted from school, stayed in his room, and refused to accept help. For the present Mrs. B., her husband's inability to take charge as a parent and mate made her feel as if he had broken an agreement he had made with her: to be an overall benevolent authority.

Mr. B.'s guilt and dependency had to be relieved if he were to give himself peace and be an effective father, husband, and ex-spouse. This required a deeper appreciation of his long-standing need not to be able to allow himself to have for himself. He finally was able to determine a limited and appropriate sense of obligations to others instead of guilt-ridden stance that dated to his "obligation" to become the man of the house after his father's death when he was 11. The present Mrs. B. recognized her "fill-the-vacuum" role. She accepted a goal of allowing Mr. B. to take charge, rather than denigrating his efforts in that direction. The former Mrs. B. refused to see the therapist with her former husband or by herself. Father and son then worked out an arrangement for the adolescent boy to meet his mother either at the home of one of her relatives or at a restaurant. The boy's increasing feelings of discomfort and guilt in regard to his own feelings required some work with him alone and with his father.

An ex-spouse and a "former life" can also intrude in the current marriage in the form of life-style differences, tastes, ideals, values, and political viewpoints, which may have been acquired through experience with and influence of the former spouse. To the extent that a new spouse identifies these as representing a predecessor's imprimatur, they can invoke jealousy, competitiveness, and resentment in the current relationship.

Sexuality and Remarriage

Just as clinicians may avoid dealing with the ex-spouse, so too they may avoid inquiring and dealing with sexuality. We find that sex is commonly better for the remarried partners than it had been in the previous relationships. This can be related to greater maturity, more experience, clarity as to sexual needs, and a better marital situation. Still, the clinician should inquire about the couple's sexuality and be able to place any sexual difficulties into perspective and determine whether sexual problems are secondary to marital difficulty, whether marital difficulty is secondary to sexual problems, or whether there is a sexual problem that predates the current relationship and ripples out to affect other areas of the couple's well-being. The current relationship may be too poor to tackle sexual problems until other areas are dealt with. These issues are discussed more completely elsewhere (2, 7).

Premarital sex is usually good for remarried couples because many partners do not elect to enter into a marriage where sex is not up to their expectations. At the start of a new relationship one or both partners may have a situational dysfunction based on guilt toward a former partner, apprehension at the thought of achieving the sought-after gratifying relationship, or uneasiness with a relative stranger. One person may experience insecurity about his or her ability to perform sexually with a new partner. The dysfunction is likely to correct itself shortly when it is situational and when the new partner is not setting off associations on some level that are reminders of unhappy experiences in the past. A single gesture, personality trait, or physical characteristic may become a symbol for the totality of the negatively viewed person or experience. Reassurance or relaxation techniques to decrease the focus on performance are often all that is necessary therapeutically.

Sex usually remains satisfactory after marriage, although frequency may decrease as the partners continue in a familiar conjugal bed and as they are faced with the problems of daily living. However, we have been impressed by the number of remarried couples who continue an active and pleasurable sexual relationship. As in any committed relationship, it is necessary to give thought, attention, and discussion to keeping sex alive and creative in a remarriage.

The incidence of incest and other forms of sexual abuse is probably higher in remarriage than in intact families (8). Stepdaughters and stepfathers are particularly at risk, even more so when the stepfather experiences nonacceptance in his spouse's family. Stepsiblings' sex play and consummation with each other is another common form of household sex. Although repetition of the Phaedra scene occurs, it is less common than stepfather-stepdaughter involvement. An increasing incidence of cases of homosexual exploitation of prepubescent, pubescent, and adolescent youths by stepparents is coming to light. The handling of these situations is beyond the scope of this article. It is important for the clinician who is inexperienced with these abuse problems to seek expert consultation. All abuse cases must be reported to the appropriate governmental agencies in each state.

VULNERABILITIES OF THE THERAPIST

The potential for counterproductive emotional and cognitive reactions in therapists varies with the general vulnerability of the therapist and with the amount of stimulation the therapeutic situation provides to the therapist's emotional and value systems. Working with remarried couples and families probably provides more such stimulation than other treatment situations. The first area of emotional assault on the therapist has to do with male-female relatedness and systems of loyalties and consanguinity. The therapist may have values markedly different from those that have allowed remarried adults to divorce and remarry, live with someone, or terminate a marriage. The actions, attitudes, and feelings of various remarried family members touch off emotional reactions based on experiences the therapist has had, has feared, or has not dared to bring about in his or her own life because of guilt, anxiety, superego constraints, or cultural considerations. More narrowly defined countertransferential reactions may also occur, wherein patients or their systems, or both, enmesh the therapist, who then reacts in the way the patient or the system unconsciously sets him up to react.

The complexities of the remarriage systems, the sense of despair, hopelessness, and loss, and the chaos and crisis that are at work may spill over into the therapist's personal life. We found ourselves putting our personal relationships on hold and avoiding decisions about making or ending personal commitments to others. Depression and despair were our common reactions, without clarity about the source of these feelings, as we witnessed our clients' despair over their life situations.

These reactions can best be dealt with through the use of a trusted and supportive group of peers. Consultation, supervision, and the use of the group to help individual therapists resolve personal reactions can mitigate some of the anxiety and pain that seem built into work with remarriage systems. We have identified the following specific areas of vulnerability for therapists working with remarriage systems.

Unrealistic Expectations. Many remarried couples marry with the hope that this marriage will right all previous relationship disappointments, including both parental and past marital failures, and that this time their marriage contract and expectations, even if unrealistic and magical, will be fulfilled. Other family members may also expect that their unmet needs will now be gratified. If the therapist accepts the unrealistic expectations, he too may be dragged down into feelings of hopelessness that so often characterize the clinical population of remarriage. Accepting these expectations will lead the clinician to become enmeshed in disappointment and disillusionment, and will lead to therapeutic paralysis and despair.

Denial. If the adult partners are pseudomutual and deny their differences, conflict, and disappointments, they are likely to focus their problems on a child or children who are scapegoated. The therapist, sensing that certain material is forbidden, may join the denial and also displace the child, thereby encouraging the pseudo-mutuality and scapegoating. Therapists may also collude with the family in their denial of the importance and relevance of their history and the suprasystem to the present problem. All too often children are told by their remarrying parent that the marriage is for the child's benefit or welfare, the parent denying his or her own needs to the child. This type of denial may arouse critical feelings within the therapist, which often are also denied and come out indirectly. The key is knowledge; the more the therapist knows about remarriage situations, the less likely he or she is to join family members in their resistance and obfuscation.

Abandonment Fears.   Loss and abandonment are prime issues for adults in remarriage, and may trigger the therapist's own abandonment anxieties.

Control Issues.   Therapists may attempt to allay their own anxiety by becoming overcontrolling, as do some harried stepparents, or by taking impulsive therapeutic action. They may rush too soon to try to impose order and consequently push the couple away. Therapists are likely to despair when the chaos does not right itself quickly in response to their interventions, and they may consciously or unconsciously dismiss the family. Ability to tolerate ambiguity and chaos is required, along with patience and awareness of the process that needs to take place during treatment.

Value Issues.   Value issues may affect unmarried, married, formerly married, and remarried therapists. For the unmarried and the married, the remarriage situation can stimulate fears of what might happen or what they might fear to do. Often such fears become defensively expressed as value judgments that bind the anxiety, as in the following situation:

Case Example 3

Dr. A. was a 55-year-old psychiatrist whose one marriage had been troubled and conflictual for many years. In working with a remarried couple consisting of an older man who left his wife and married a younger woman, the therapist found himself secretly relishing the couple's marital problems. "He deserves what he got," thought Dr. A. This judgment made him feel more comfortable. He had often fantasized about leaving his wife but felt it would be morally wrong.

Clients and their therapists all too often fall into trying to make the myth come true that the new marriage and family will literally reconstitute a perfect marriage and family. Sometimes they may even want to pick up from where the first marriage turned sour. They now seek to replace their spouse with a new one who will carry on from where the other had started to fail them. They continue to pursue an impossible dream.

The complexity of the remarriage system when either partner has young children does put remarriages at greater risk than first marriages. When the remarriage is dysfunctional, the sense of despair and loss, the disorganization, and the never-ending series of emergencies may affect therapists so that they too become loaded down with despair. When this happens we have taken on the load of the couple's mental state and become equally ineffective. Reviewing goals to establish small, incremental aims that are possible to achieve is usually a more appropriate approach than going along with the goal of becoming an idealized intact family.

Misdiagnosis. Owing to the heightened emotionality manifested by some remarried couples as they see their second-chance hope for a happy marriage and family life disappearing, the stress may cause them to react in ways that appear to be disproportionately abnormal. It is easy for therapists to misdiagnose individual psychopathology and to designate a diagnosis more serious than the accurate one. In these situations relief of stress may be the first priority of marital therapy; for example, consolidation of the marital relationship, time spent away from the children, or relief of guilt about not loving a stepchild.

Support Groups for Therapists

All too many mental health facilities, under pressure to increase productivity, fail to offer time or encouragement to staff professionals who work with remarried couples and who wish to arrange conferences in order to form a support group for one another. There must be security of confidentiality and separation from administrative censure of any form if therapists are to be able to deal with their personal reactions.

For all those in private practice who have completed formal training, it is important to have a place where cases, feelings, and new ideas can be discussed. For most people this is best done in a peer group. No therapist can function very long without feedback from colleagues. Patients' opinions are not sufficient to prevent our occupational disease of depression and/or grandiosity. It is essential to have peer supervision in which countertransferential matters can be brought to the therapist's attention in a constructive fashion, new ideas can be discussed, and some therapy may even be done (so long as the lattermost is an agreed-upon function of the group).

Extensive educational and self-help group work is continuing to help prevent breakdown of second marriages; however, space does not allow us to deal with this work here. Emily and John Visher have made monumental contributions to this area (9). We have reviewed our work elsewhere (4).

The approach to treating the remarried couples described here is not the final word by any means. It is a flexible approach providing a theoretical system and methodology that allows therapists a great deal of individual initiative. This system of therapy usually calls for one therapist; however, as in all therapy, that therapist requires the support of colleagues in some form of peer-group supervision. The more diverse the professional, theoretical, and experiential backgrounds of the group, the more likely it is that therapists will constantly review their work and continue to improve the quality of their endeavors.

The remarried couple has been the focus of this chapter. However, it is important to remember that children, ex-spouses, and other members of the remarried suprafamily must often be seen in the assessment phase and/or at various times during the course of treatment.

References

1. Pasley K, Ihinger-Tallman M: Remarried Family Life Supports and Constraints, in Family Strengths 4: Positive Support Systems. Edited by Stinnett N, et al. Lincoln, University of Nebraska Press, 1982

2. Sager CJ: Marriage Contracts and Couple Therapy: Hidden Forces in Intimate Relationships. New York, Brunner/Mazel, 1976

3. Sager CJ: Couples therapy and marriage contracts, in Handbook of Family Therapy. Edited by Gurman AS, Kniskern DP. New York, Brunner/Mazel, 1981

4. Sager CJ, Brown HS, Crohn H, et al: Treating the Remarried Family. New York, Brunner/Mazel, 1983

5. Berne E: Transactional Analysis in Psychotherapy. New York, Grove Press, 1961

6. Carter FS, McGoldrick M: The Family Life Cycle: A Framework for Family Therapy. New York, Gardner Press, 1980

7. Sager CJ: Treatment of remarried families: demography and outcome. Journal of Jewish Communal Services 60:230–238, 1984

8. Perlmutter LH, Engel T, Sager CJ: The incest taboo: loosened sexual boundaries in remarried families. J Sex Marital Ther 8: 83–106, 1982

9. Visher E, Visher J: Stepfamilies. New York, Brunner/Mazel, 1979

Appendix

REMINDER LIST FOR MARRIAGE CONTRACT— REMARRIAGE

Marriage contract, as the term is used here, does not refer to formal contracts or agreements that both mates write out and subscribe to openly. The contract, as referred to here, consists of conscious and unconscious expectations of what you will give and what you wish to receive from your partner. You each have your own contract that probably differs from the other. Do not be surprised if your contract is inconsistent because you simultaneously may have strong contradictory wishes or needs. For example, you may have the desire to be independent and yet at the same time also require your spouse's approval of your actions. Such apparent contradictions are usual for most of us. If one or both of you have children from a previous marriage, you are marrying into a new type of family—you are not making a commitment just to one other person who has no important responsibilities to anyone else.

Each contract has three levels of awareness:

1. *Verbalized*—those aspects that are discussed with each other, although not always heard by the receiver.
2. *Conscious but not verbalized*—the parts of your contract that you are aware of but do not verbalize to your spouse because you fear his or her anger or disapproval, you feel embarrassed, etc.
3. *Beyond awareness or unconscious*—aspects that are beyond your usual awareness. You may have an idea of what some of these are. They are often felt as a warning light in your head or a feeling of concern that gets pushed away. Do the best you can with these.

Each person acts as if the other knew the terms of the contract (which were never really agreed upon) and feels angered, hurt, betrayed, etc., when they believe their spouse did not fulfill their part of the contract. In each area note down where you feel your needs are being met and are not being met.

Contractual terms, that is, desires, expectations, and what you are *willing to give* as well as want from marriage and your mate, fall into three general categories. The reminder list that follows consists of these three categories; following under each are listed several common areas that are sources of marital and personal trouble. Some you may have thought of before, others not.

EXPLANATION OF REMINDER LIST FOR MARRIAGE CONTRACT—REMARRIAGE

The following is a guide to help you respond to the questions. Do not compare with your spouse until *after* you both have completed your own.

1. Respond to all areas that are meaningful to you.
2. Answer in terms of today. If something is a sore point from the past indicate this.
3. Make your answers as long or as short as you wish, but if they are to be useful they must convey your feelings, not just "yes" or "no."
4. Do not try to do all these three categories at one time. One at a sitting is recommended.

Name _____ Date _____

This is your (circle)	1st	2nd	3rd Marriage
Your partner's (circle)	1st	2nd	3rd Marriage

Length of current relationship Years _____ months _____

For you: years _____ and months _____ since separation.
        years _____ and months _____ since divorce.

For mate: years _____ and months _____ since separation.
        years _____ and months _____ since divorce.

I bring the following child(ren) to this household:
Name _____ M F Age ___ Lives with us _ Visits ___
Name _____ M F Age ___ Lives with us _ Visits ___
Name _____ M F Age ___ Lives with us _ Visits ___

My partner brings the following child(ren) to this household:
Name _____ M F Age ___ Lives with us _ Visits ___
Name _____ M F Age ___ Lives with us _ Visits ___
Name _____ M F Age ___ Lives with us _ Visits ___

We have the following child(ren) together:
Name _____ M F Age ___
Name _____ M F Age ___

1. CATEGORIES BASED ON EXPECTATIONS OF MARRIAGE

Each partner lives with or marries for his or her own purposes and goals in relation to coupling. The couples system itself generates other purposes and goals of which the individuals may have been unaware originally. Keep in mind that this list is meant only to remind you to consider these possibilities. Others may be important for you; if so, include them. When "marriage" is stated, living together without the legality of marriage is included as an alternative. This area relates to each person's purposes and goals in relation to the institution of marriage itself and what you are willing to contribute and what you believe is your mate's position. Please write out a summary of what you *want* from your marriage that relates to the above areas, and what *in exchange* you will *give*. The most common expectations of marriage, as related to remarriage are:

1. A mate who will be loyal, devoted, and exclusive. A relationship with a person that is very like the first mate when "things were good," or that will provide what the first mate didn't. To have romantic love and intimacy.
2. Help in dealing with, caring for, and disciplining the children.

3. Companionship and insurance against loneliness. A relief from the world of the formerly married, the single parent, or the single person.
4. To be rescued from responsibilities and burdens. To return to the "order" and "certitude" of marriage and the two-parent family.
5. A relationship till death do us part. There may be a grim determination or pressure to make the marriage work this time.
6. Sanctioned and readily available sex. Escape from the pressures of dating. Sex which is legitimate in the eyes of the children and an example of values you wish to transmit as a parent or stepparent.
7. To have children with your new mate.
8. A relationship that emphasizes parenting and family life.
9. A relationship in which my spouse and I can devote ourselves to each other primarily.
10. A family and economic unit where possessions and financial resources will be shared or will not be shared.
11. To have an immediate ready-made family.
12. To be taken care of myself by a strong-appearing motherly or fatherly person.
13. To prove your desirability and superiority as a spouse to your partner's former mate, and/or your own former mate.
14. To rescue an apparently struggling person and perhaps his or her children.
15. Others—list and discuss.

2. CATEGORIES BASED ON PSYCHOLOGICAL AND BIOLOGICAL NEEDS

These parameters are important because it is here that your mate is expected to fulfill your needs directly. They arise largely from within you and your interaction with your partner. The needs and desires by which these factors may be expressed often are beyond your awareness, yet you do have some ideas about them. Write out a summary of what you *want* from your mate that relates to the following items and what *in exchange* you will *give*. The reciprocal nature of these contracts is especially important here. Some of the most common areas that require consideration and awareness are:

1. *Adaptations and ties to your own children.* Do you recognize the need to alter an overly close bond with your child that developed during the single-parent stage? Can your new mate be helpful in understanding your relationship with your child? Does your new mate react by feeling excluded, jealous, or angry? Vice-versa in reference to your mate's children and what you expect.

2. *Ties to former spouse.* Are you aware of residual, appropriate or inappropriate feelings of affection, hostility, or revenge for the former spouse? Do these feelings and/or actions affect your relationship? Do you say provocative things to arouse jealousy between your former and current spouse, or does your current spouse do so? Respond to the same questions regarding your spouse and his/her former mate, if appropriate.

3. *Independence-dependence.* What degree and type of independence do you want for yourself and your mate?

4. *Closeness-distance.* Communication problems are often related to the ability or inability to tolerate closeness. How much space and time alone do you need? Is there a reaction in this marriage that relates to the past; for example, a fear of risking too much closeness again or a demand for closeness that wasn't present in the first marriage? To what extent do you or your mate's children and their needs come between you and your mate?

5. *Use-abuse of power.* Distribution of power. How much power and control do you need? How is your need for power different or similar to that in your first marriage? Do you or your mate abuse power; can you share power? How does it work for you two?

6. *Decision making.* How and by whom are decisions made?

7. *Guilt.* Does guilt toward your former spouse, children, your parents, ex-in-laws, or religious beliefs affect or color what you

wish to or feel you can or should give in your new marriage?
Does your spouse have problems surrounding guilt or lack of
guilt that bother you? Is he or she too feeling/unfeeling or
responsible/irresponsible in regard to his/her children, ex-
spouse, or you?

8. *Roles.* What does each partner expect their role to be as stepparent or parent to their visiting or custodial child? What does
each spouse expect from the other in this regard? How does
one expect and desire co-parenting to work for the two biological parents and the stepparents?

9. *Fear of loneliness or abandonment.* To what extent does the
fear of another loss or abandonment play a role in this marriage? Is this a fear you have always had?

10. *Level of anxiety.* To what extent are you fearful of another
failure, repetition of old patterns, and/or that the new mate
will show evidence of acting like the former? On a scale of 1 to
5, with 1 no anxiety and 5 frequent and overwhelming anxiety, where do you rate your anxiety level? Circle the appropriate number.

Yours:	1	2	3	4	5
Your Mate's:	1	2	3	4	5

11. *Nurturing/affection.* How would you like affection, love, and
consideration to be shown to you, and how would you like to
express it to your partner? For example, do you like physical
affection, thoughtfulness, kind words, gifts, and/or consideration of your sensitivities and idiosyncrasies? Is there anything
that you or your partner feel or do that makes expressing
affection difficult?

12. Are these problems arising from where you and your spouse
are in your life cycle? For example, does one want children but
other does not because he/she has children; or does one want
to cut down on work while the other is at the start of a career
he/she wants to pursue?

13. *Characteristics desired in your partner.* These may include
sex, personality, physical appearance, expressiveness, achieve-

ment level, giving and receiving love, tenderness, ability to function socially, at work or as family members, and other parameters. Do these relate to characteristics of your first mate either directly or indirectly?

14. *Acceptance of self and other.* Does each of you have the ability to love yourself as well as the other? Is love equated with vulnerability? Did you or your spouse "love" in the first marriage and now see love as dangerous?

15. *Cognitive style.* This refers to the way in which you and your mate take information in, process it, arrive at decisions, and communicate the process and conclusions to the other. Are intelligence and conceptualization levels compatible? Is there a positive complementarity of differences or do these cause dissonance?

16. Are your interests and those of your mate the same? Do you feel that most interests should be similar?

17. Add any other areas not mentioned.

18. Please write out a summary of what you *want* from your mate that relates to the above categories and what *in exchange* you will *give.*

3. EXTERNAL FOCI OF MARITAL PROBLEMS

These are common areas of complaints that many couples have. They may appear to be the core of the marital or family problems; however, more often they are the *external manifestations* of problems that are rooted in the first two categories. Write a summary of what you *want* in regard to the above expectations and what you will *give in exchange.* The most common manifestations are:

1. *Communication.* To what extent can you be open with one another? As a couple can you talk, listen, and understand each other? Can a satisfactory conclusion be reached by discussing disagreements?

2. *Life-styles.* To what extent are your life-styles and cultures similar? Do you make comparisons to life-styles or cultures of

your former marriage and family? Are there problems stemming from this area?

3. *Families of origin.* Does one partner resent the other's family or the mate's involvement with them? Did your parents or your spouse's take a major role before remarriage that causes problems now?

4. *Relations with ex-spouse and ex-in-laws.* How involved is each mate with the former spouse, how friendly or hostile? How does that affect the current relationship? What role should each of you have with his/her former spouse and in-laws?

5. *Child rearing.* To what extent do you agree on how to raise the children, how much authority to exercise, how much leniency, and how will caretaking be shared?

6. *Relationship with children.* How does each relate to the other's and their own children, both living-in and visiting? Anything you would like to see changed?

7. *Family myths.* Do partners collaborate in the maintenance of myths; for example, that the remarried family is perfect and harmonious? Is anyone idealized or are there family "secrets?"

8. *Money.* How is it controlled? Is it kept separate or combined? Does one partner feel cheated because of the economic obligations to the other's spouse or children? How are resources from the present marriage, from a former marriage, and inherited monies and property allocated in wills? Do older children resent a parent's new spouse as "stealing" their inheritance?

9. *Milestones.* What are expectations regarding who in the remarried and other biological parent's household will attend children's celebrations—birthdays, graduations, bar mitzvahs, confirmations, and weddings? How are children expected to spend holidays—Christmas, Thanksgiving, summers, etc.?

10. *Sexuality.* Attitudes and predilections may differ in frequency, forms of pleasuring, fidelity, expectations, initiation, openness with children about sexuality, etc. How is this dealt with by the adults and with children?

11. *Values.* Is there general agreement on priorities such as money, culture, ethics, relations with others, religion, use of time together? How are differences of values and culture between two biological parent households handled?

12. *Friends.* What is the attitude toward the other's friends? Can each tolerate the other's friends from former relationships? Do all friends have to be joint, or can each have individual friendships? How much time should be for friends and how much as a couple? Are opposite-gender friends as acceptable as same-gender?

13. *Housing.* Are there problems arising from continuing use of your home or your mate's as your common home; same for furnishings? Any problems related to space for children or for yourself or spouse?

14. Add any subjects you deem significant.

15. FINAL QUESTION: add any additional comments or thoughts about yourself, your mate, the children, your marriage and remarriage that occur to you.

5

An Integrative Approach to Couples Therapy

Derek C. Polonsky, M.D.
Carol C. Nadelson, M.D.

5

An Integrative Approach to Couples Therapy

Interest in couples therapy has grown considerably over the past several decades and has led to the development of both theory and practice. When one considers some of the issues raised by Drs. Stewart, Bjorksten, and Glick in Chapter 1 of this monograph with regard to the enormous flux that is occurring within couples and families and that affects roughly 90 percent of the population, one can understand why couples therapy has grown in importance. With the rise in the incidence of divorce and with the high rate of remarriage following it, more couples have been confronted with the disappointing reality that similar problems often recur in the second marriage. We believe that couples, rather than divorcing again, are requesting joint therapy as a means of saving and healing their marriages.

It has impressed us how often clinicians have approached their work as an innovation rather than an extension of previous work. Newly proposed theories have often been described as different when in reality they may reflect only subtle differences with past contributions. Our sense is that the wheel has been repeatedly rediscovered. In this chapter we will not review the major theoretical positions with regard to couples therapy, since we assume the reader is familiar with them. Rather, we will suggest ways in which therapists can integrate different therapeutic models to deal most effectively with changing clinical realities.

Generally, one's therapeutic perspective reflects the approach emphasized in one's training. Whether one favors psychodynamic, systems, or behavioral therapy is often a reflection of past experience and comfort rather than the integration of new information or understanding. Our own route followed training in individual psychoanalytically oriented psychotherapy.

We were impressed with the repeated observation that some patients in individual psychotherapy who focused initially on intrapsychic issues began to focus almost exclusively on difficulties in their dyadic relationships, whether long-term marriages or long-term unmarried relationships. The form this took varied: some patients would repeatedly present themselves as victims; some complained that the partner could do more or be different but were never satisfied by the partner's efforts; some produced material that repeatedly conveyed a sense of not being understood *and* not understanding. What was important was the subtle but relentless change in the focus of the material. Gradually, most therapy hours became oriented around some aspect of the relationship with the significant other person, and we wondered whether couples therapy would be a more effective approach.

Therapists often become advocates for their patients, so the therapeutic relationship, so necessary in individual psychotherapy, may interfere with a patient's ability to deal with his or her own interpersonal issues. Partners and therapist alike may be unaware that this is occurring. The therapist's support may hamper the integration of ambivalent feelings and inadvertently foster splitting. Martin and Bird (1) attempted to address this issue in what they call stereoscopic therapy. In this form, each of the two therapists saw one partner of a couple, and then the therapists collaborated to understand the "reality." This early attempt at couples therapy addressed reality, but not the meaning of misperception and miscommunication. Individually oriented therapists have maintained a degree of skepticism about what can be accomplished in couples therapy because of the specific nature of transference and countertransference processes within a dyad. Object relations theory (2) and the concept of projective identification (3, 4), however, have contributed substantially to an elaboration and integration of an approach to couples therapy and have addressed the issue of why partners who profess enormous anger and dislike for each other remain together. These perspectives suggest that it is helpful to understand each partner's history and dynamics before they are brought together into the interpersonal system.

In the evaluative meetings, each partner is initially seen alone. During this meeting, an attempt is made to understand the individual psychodynamics and to formulate issues that may be recreated in the marital relationship. It is also necessary to assess motivation for therapy, as well as for the relationship. The couple is then seen together to understand their interaction.

The first phase of the treatment usually involves clarification of 1) the *intent* of each partner, 2) their *perceptions* of the relationship, and 3) differences in their *styles* of relating. Couples frequently report that they experience a diminished sense of tension as this process occurs. The nature of the object relationships of each partner begins to be elucidated both from what they reveal about their interactions and from the development of the transference. Often couples begin to expose issues that they initially were unable to report. For the therapist, changes of facial expression or tone of voice, even unacknowledged by one or the other partner, may represent important clues. The therapist may question what has been observed, and the couple may begin to notice more of the subtleties of their interaction.

Case Example 1

Dr. and Mrs. R. had been seen as a couple for a while. At one meeting, they arrived at different times, and the wife flew into the therapist's office and demanded, "Where is Rick?" Before the therapist could answer, she turned around and stormed back into the waiting room. The husband had been in the bathroom, and came into the office. The wife then returned and stood at the door, glowered at the husband and said, "Where were you?" The husband meekly said he was in the bathroom, and the two then began to talk about something that had happened during the week. The therapist interrupted the couple and asked about what had just happened. He asked the wife if she was angry with the husband when he was not found in the therapist's office. She was surprised and denied it. However, this led to an important discussion about how nonverbal signals affected their experience of each other.

There are times when material may come up in a couple's session which points to a particular issue in one individual requiring the therapist to transiently shift the focus of the sessions to attend to it. During this period, the therapy becomes individually focused while the other partner observes and helpfully contributes.

Case Example 2

A couple was talking about the anger and distance each felt during a febrile illness the husband had contracted. The wife felt shut out and, at the same time, the object of considerable anger. An exploration of the situation revealed that the husband's early family experience was relevant. When he was very young, he had been left for several months when his parents went abroad to do research. He recounted some of his childhood experiences of being ill, and how he felt abandoned, helpless, and rageful. He became aware that he was re-enacting this with his wife. During the course of one session, he was able to articulate his feelings about his earlier experience and see the origin of the intensity of his current reactions. His wife, in understanding more about his earlier experience, was able to feel less angry, more empathic, and less guilty and responsible for his response.

In this example, the change in focus to individual issues permitted both partners to learn more about the inner experience of the husband. This represents another level of the communication clarification process wherein earlier experiences are connected with current affects. There is the risk that the partner toward whom particular attention is being focused will feel characterized as the sick one. This perception must be addressed early, and the partner should be encouraged to share his or her feelings about being in this position. At times, similar attention to issues for the other partner may allow each to feel more support and understanding. This issue, however, can become more complex if one partner has a more overt and problematic psychopathology. For example, if one partner has a borderline character structure and employs projection, splitting, and externalization, the therapist may initially have to expend considerable therapeutic effort working on these mechanisms in order that the individual can begin to "own" some of the projected affects and impulses.

However, the therapist must be mindful that in the marital dyad there are powerful unconscious collusive processes. The therapist has to guard against inadvertently joining these collusions of perception in which the supposedly sicker spouse is identified as the person needing modification, and the supposedly healthier spouse is seen as the long-suffering burdened bystander. The unconscious gratifications of the supposedly healthier spouse may not be evident for some time.

Case Example 3

Mr. and Mrs. B. had been married for eight years. The husband sought therapy because he viewed his wife as reluctant to be intimate and caring in a relationship. He had been involved in intensive therapy for many years, working through a very difficult childhood with a rejecting critical father and a mother who was an alcoholic and intermittently psychotic. While the husband focused on the wife's reluctance to be more intimate, he had great difficulty in recognizing the way in which he was rejecting and how he stifled any opportunity for intimacy. He was unable to see not only the way he had isolated anger but also the negative feelings he had toward his own family, which he had projected onto his wife. Further, he insisted on frequent visits to his family despite the bitter conflict this produced with his family. His wife would go along with him, although they invariably had a miserable time. The therapy was focused initially on clarifying the discrepancies between what he said he wanted (intimacy) and the way in which his actions precluded it. His individual therapy, while helpful in many ways, was not able to address the way he elicited behavior in his wife that confirmed his introjected connection with his parents.

The husband often felt that the therapist and the wife focused on him as the crazy person. Indeed, much of the time in therapy was spent on trying to understand the nature of what he wanted from his wife and of his distorted perception. The therapist encouraged him to verbalize his feelings of being ganged up on. His wife talked about how he had similar feelings in two previous courses of couples' therapy. The degree to which he excluded his wife precluded examination of her difficulties. Clearly, she had chosen a man who was emotionally isolated and who could not tolerate intimacy. But the intensity of his distortion so colored their interaction that it was not possible to see the wife's role in it.

This kind of situation is clinically complex. The therapist may be forced temporarily to compromise a direct therapeutic approach because of the intensity of the "sicker" partner's response (that is, the therapist may have to give up pursuing some of the intense externalizations and projections, because to continue this confrontation would so threaten the individual that he or she would leave treatment). This is analogous to the stance in individual therapy in which the therapist may delay a confrontation or interpretation out of concern that the patient's defenses would not tolerate it.

Case Example 4

Mr. and Mrs. P. requested therapy because of their intensifying anger and "inability to communicate." From the individual meeting with Mrs. P., the therapist decided that she had a borderline character structure with the need to project and externalize. She also demonstrated some paranoid features under stress. From the individual meeting with Mr. P., the therapist felt that he was quite narcissistic, though he functioned in a less divisive paranoid way. It was repeatedly noted that the couple would deal with a particular issue and would just approach a point of resolution when the wife would throw a curve ball, which was not relevant to the matter at hand but would serve to anger and infuriate the husband. At this point she would sit back, throw up her hands, look at the therapist, and say, "You see how he will not deal with any of the real issues." After a few attempts at clarifying the extent of her inability to take responsibility for her own feelings, the therapist became concerned about her feeling paranoid and unsupported in the treatment and so decided to delay the work or at least attenuate the confrontations. An attempt was made to keep a ledger-like balance on how much time was focused on each individual with the hope that gradually attention could be directed to the serious difficulty that the wife had in owning her affects.

Increasingly, couples present with a request for sexual therapy rather than marital therapy. They appear to be more comfortable acknowledging sexual problems than marital discord (5). The couple's therapist is presented with a particular challenge in assessing the nature and etiology of the sexual complaint and integrating it into couples therapy. Often, couples will initially indicate that they do not want a long talking-therapy approach and that they have read about sex therapy and that is precisely what they need. In our experience, few couples (about 10 percent) have purely sexual issues that could be addressed by a sex-therapy approach alone. After a few sessions, the majority of patients who present with a sexual complaint will come to an understanding of the complexity of their difficulties. For many, there is a defensive need to see their problem as sexual, and they therefore resist considering the importance of relationship issues. In these situations, it is often effective to accede initially to the request for sex therapy in order to establish an alliance. The fantasy often held by couples is that sex therapy is a formula that does not require much emotional involvement and that they can be plugged in and turned out fixed. Often after a brief time (one or two sessions), resistance emerges which is usually manifested by noncompletion of the sensate-focus exercises. This occurs because the partners are unable to communicate, are too angry with each other, or are uncomfortable with the intimacy or affect generated by this degree of closeness. After this experience most couples are more amenable to discussing the more difficult aspects of their marriage and will engage in a more comprehensive couples therapy.

There are couples who initially identify the problem as sexual but who are able to hear that there are also problems in their relationship that require attention.

Case Example 5

Mr. and Mrs. C. sought sex therapy because Mr. C. had diminished sexual desire. Mrs. C. observed that early in their marriage her hus-

band seemed less interested in sex than she was. He readily complied
with her request for more sex, only to tell her months later that he felt
burdened, coerced, and resentful. Mrs. C., in the course of the evaluation, also complained about their struggles over how much time he
worked. Again he felt coerced, and although he complied, he was
resentful and angry. The therapist pointed out his repeated experience
of being coerced and his subsequent response of feeling angry. When it
was suggested that to focus on the sexual problems would be to ignore
these feelings, the couple agreed to couples therapy focusing beyond
the sexual issues.

Sager (6), in reflecting on the evolution in his thinking about
the role of the therapist in treating couples with sexual problems,
stated that he initially believed that one needed to keep sexual and
couples therapy separate but later reversed his view and proposed
that the couples therapist ought to be versed in the techniques of
sexual therapy and be ready to shift the focus when indicated
rather than refer patients to another "sexual" therapist. This cer-
tainly agrees with our own clinical experience. Since many couples use their sexual activity as a metaphor for their relationship,
only by integrating sexual and marital treatment can the therapist
fully engage the couple. By being able to deal effectively with
unconscious issues, interpersonal dynamics, and sexual issues, the
therapist is in a position to reinforce the integration of sexuality
into marital interactions. Furthermore, since the therapeutic relationship develops over time, it takes several months for a couple to
feel trusting enough to reveal deeper issues. Once they have exposed their vulnerabilities, it is difficult to imagine justifying a
referral to another therapist because a sexual problem arises or a
marital problem comes up.

A related phenomenon occurs when couples therapy is used as
the vehicle for a person to obtain individual therapy. A couple
may request therapy for general marital complaints, such as failure to communicate, and as the therapy proceeds, one partner may
tend to focus on individual issues. The spouse adds some perspective, but the focus of the therapy moves away from the marriage.
The "patient" in the couple may have felt too threatened to seek
individual therapy independently and may have needed the pro-

tection of the spouse to allow this to occur. We have found that a change in the therapist's role from conjoint to individual therapy may be effective.

Case Example 6

Mr. and Mrs. P. came for couples therapy stating that they were having difficulty communicating and were feeling increasingly distant. In the initial interviews, the husband revealed himself to be an extremely frightened and vulnerable man. What had initially appeared as anger was now understood as terror. As the sessions proceeded, it became clear that there was virtually no area in which he felt safe and secure. He felt attacked and vulnerable, and he retreated defensively. The use of his vocabulary was particularly revealing. He would, for example, use comments such as "you 'hit' me with that remark." After a few months of therapy, the therapist recommended individual therapy for Mr. P. in addition to the couples therapy.

Here, the couples therapist is faced with the question of whether to continue couples therapy, in addition to recommending individual therapy, or whether to suggest putting the couples therapy on hold for a while. Our experience is that by discussing the choices and their implications with the couple (individual therapy with another therapist but no couples therapy, individual therapy with couples therapist but no couples therapy, or individual therapy with couples therapist and couples therapy) the therapist and patients may jointly arrive at a decision about which course to follow.

A variant of this is when one partner has a bipolar illness. Couples therapy can have added value over individual therapy because of the input from the spouse regarding the subtle early changes of behavior that the affected spouse may not report. Given that the mood swings seem unrelated to current events, it is particularly disruptive to a marital relationship when the affect of one partner dramatically changes. Our experience is that the spouse often feels confused and struggles to find some rational explanation for the change, sometimes even holding himself or herself responsible. In this setting, couples therapy provides an opportunity both to follow the course of affective changes with an objective observer and to help the spouse understand and deal with the changes this produces.

Case Example 7

Mr. and Mrs. D. were referred for an evaluation by a gynecologist. The couple sought her out for help with a sexual complaint, but the gynecologist was concerned about the husband's mental status, and wanted a consultation. The husband was clearly in the midst of a manic episode, with inappropriate behavior, poor reality testing, hyperactivity, and grandiose ideas with regard to money. By the husband's account, nothing was wrong, and he could make a convincing case to explain all of his behavior. However, the wife was able to provide some objectivity and, in particular, to talk about the way he was different now compared with previously. The couple was seen while the husband was placed on medication, and the joint meetings focused on the changes in his behavior and the effects of the medication. When the acute symptoms were treated, the couple were able to look at the interpersonal difficulties in their relationship. Later in the course of the therapy, the wife described some changes in the husband's behavior (getting up early, getting involved in palm reading) which alerted the therapist to another manic episode. Medication was prescribed early, and the ravages of the previous manic episodes were avoided.

During the course of couples therapy, as the therapist learns more about the families of origin and each partner's early experience, the therapist might gain insight into the nature of the dynamics of the couple's present family. The meaning of some of the interactions with the couple's children may become evident, and the therapist might suggest a few family meetings to attempt to help the couple and their children deal more effectively with each other.

Case Example 8

Mr. and Mrs. B. had been in couples therapy for some years. They had an emotionally intense relationship, in which they both expressed much anger, and had great difficulty in tolerating closeness. Each felt rejected and unsupported by the other. Gradually, more was learned about each of their families of origin. The wife's father developed a presenile dementia, and her mother was so overwhelmed by this stress that she was not able to attend to her daughter's needs. The husband had a father who was extremely violent and eventually abandoned his family and a mother who had repeated extramarital affairs and a serious drinking problem.

As the couple began to understand and own their feelings about their families of origin, they were able to see how they reenacted them with each other; each felt some relief. Trust in the therapist improved, and they were able to talk about the difficulties they were having with their own children. What gradually emerged was that neither partner felt cared for in the family.

The therapist suggested a few family meetings. In them, each of the two daughters talked about how they felt left out, and one in particular felt uncared for. The parents were genuinely surprised to hear this and were able to share with the children some of their own experiences in their families that were similar and about which they felt sad. In the course of these sessions, the family was able to share their sense of sadness and loss and were able to modify their behavior, respond more positively to each other, and feel more cared for.

Next, we will consider the role of the therapist once a couple has decided to split. If marital therapy has continued for several years, the therapist may have to deal with countertransference feelings related to this marital and/or therapeutic "failure." However, the therapist may be in a unique position to help the couple as they begin to disengage. During the therapy, the dynamics of the relationship may have become clearer, and the therapist can have an important role in identifying salient issues and helping the couple mourn their relationship rather than mask these feelings with anger. The therapist can also be of enormous value in actively guiding the couple with regard to issues surrounding children, even providing suggestions about how to talk to them and how to make childcare arrangements in the immediate and subsequent periods. Wallerstein (7) has studied the long-term effects of separation and divorce on children. She describes some of the initial reactions of children to learning about the separation and discusses factors that appear to make the split easier or more difficult for them to handle. In particular, she has observed that the single most important factor is that the departing parent remain consistently involved and available to the children. When the departing parent moves away and does not remain involved, the effects on the children in terms of depression are most noticeable. For some couples, divorce may be a therapeutic success rather than a therapeutic failure. For many couples, divorce therapy has helped them think through their expectations of their relationships and define what they felt to be lacking. They may have reached a point where they realized that the marriage will simply not provide what they want and feel that they are freer to end it.

CONCLUSION

We would like to reaffirm our view that couples therapy provides a very effective means of addressing difficult interpersonal issues in a unique and powerful way. We have struggled over the years to bring together our understanding about individual therapy, including the usefulness of the transference to uncover hidden motivations and affects, with principles of couples therapy. Couples therapy is initially anxiety provoking for both therapist and couple. For the therapist, there is the need to get to know two individuals simultaneously and at the same time to sort out the complexities of their interpersonal relationships. For the couple, there is the anxiety of being unable to hide effectively from the therapist.

In our work with couples, we have been impressed with the need to be flexible in our therapeutic approach and have elaborated several situations in which this flexibility is necessary. In summary, these situations arise on the following occasions:

1. When in the course of couples therapy an issue arises with one partner that requires a transient shift to individual therapy within the couples therapy.
2. When the partners collude with each other such that one is viewed as the sicker, more pathologic partner. The therapist needs to clarify the role of the supposedly healthier partner in perpetuating this collusion and determine the benefit each partner derives from it.
3. When one partner actually has a significantly more psycho-

pathological condition. In such a situation the therapist may
need to compromise dealing directly with those issues in the
service of attending to the therapeutic relationship, hoping
gradually to establish an alliance that would allow for more
direct confrontation of the difficulties.
4. When couples present with sexual issues, the overall relationship needs to be carefully evaluated. The issue may be primarily sexual, or the issue may not be primarily sexual but a
metaphor for the relationship, or the issue may not be primarily sexual, but treatment of a sexual problem is the only way in
which the couple is prepared to enter therapy.
5. When one partner needs to use couples therapy as the initial
way of getting into individual therapy.
6. When family meetings are needed to extend the couples work
to include other family members, such as children.

In our work with couples, we stress the importance of understanding unconscious collusions and the reenactments of early
object relationships. An attempt is made early on to introduce
these ideas to couples and to enlist their help in unraveling the
ways each partner may recreate aspects of his or her relationship
with the family of origin. In this chapter, we have attempted to
provide a link between a theoretical understanding of marital
dynamics and a variety of technical approaches.

References

1. Martin PA, Bird HW: An approach to the psychotherapy of marriage
   partners. Psychiatry 16:123–127, 1953

2. Dicks HV: Concepts of marital diagnosis and therapy as developed at
   the Tavistock family psychiatry units, in Marriage Counselling in
   Medical Practice. Edited by Nash E, Jessner L, Abse D. Chapel Hill,
   University of North Carolina Press, 1964

3. Main T: Mutual projection in marriage. Compr Psychiatry 7:432–449,
   1966

4. Zinner J: The implication of projective identification for marital interaction, in Contemporary Marriage. Edited by Grunebaum H, Christ J. Boston, Little, Brown and Co, 1976

5. Polonsky DC, Nadelson CC: Marital discord and the wish for sex therapy. Psychiatric Annals 12:685–695, 1982

6. Sager CJ: The role of sex therapy in marital therapy. Am J Psychiatry 133:555–558, 1976

7. Wallerstein J: The impact of divorce on children. Psychiatr Clin North Am 3:455–468, 1980